disconnected

technology addiction & the search for

authenticity in virtual life

dr. nicole m. radziwill

Epilogue

(yes, I know it's at the front – and yes, it's supposed to be)

"Back in the 1800s, Henry David Thoreau wrote that the man who constantly and desperately keeps going to the post office to check for correspondence from others 'has not heard from himself in a long while.' [The new book entitled] Hamlet's BlackBerry argues that the same can be said these days for those who are doing the modern equivalent: incessantly checking e-mail, Facebook, Twitter and the like.

'Of the two mental worlds everyone inhabits, the inner and the outer, the latter increasingly rules,' writes author William Powers. 'We're like so many pinballs bouncing around a world of blinking lights and buzzers. There's lots of movement and noise, but it doesn't add up to much.' Powers extols the benefits of solitude and the dangers of external validation. ('Who's read my latest post? Are there any comments on my comments? Who's paying attention to me now?')

Rasha Madkour (Associated Press), "Too Much Technology Bad for Self, Society" (7/11/2010)

Disconnected is the story of my detachment from buzz and correspondence, and is a reflection of having been disconnected within myself. As a result, it recounts the tale of my psychological unraveling. It's also the story of connecting with Self, continuously improving the Self, and using the insights gained in doing

iii

so to improve the *quality of life* for you and for those around you. Although this all started as an experiment, in retrospect I realize that eschewing the connections of social media (and later, drawing down even more) was a defense mechanism. I could no longer manage the buzz and chatter and noise of the virtual world around me, physically and emotionally stretching me to the limits I was in the process of discovering and defining. Something had to give.

I gave up technology in a last ditch effort to preserve what was left of my fractured soul. Fortunately, under the fractures, I was thankfully more intact than I ever could have recognized at first. Had I not embarked on this journey, had I not been a professor on summer teaching hiatus with the remarkable luxury of extensive "time off" – I am fairly certain that 1) I would not have been compelled to begin or complete this experiment, or 2) I would have ended up on some sort of short term disability leave from work. My mental and emotional faculties (no pun intended) were debilitated, my ability to focus on or pay attention to things around me, absent.

My purpose is to take you on an unscripted, unedited stream-of-consciousness journey that unfolded on paper, written by hand. I am not advocating technological asceticism or prescribing behavior that I think would make *you* happier. This is a journey to find the soul, to capture an authentic existence where technology and social media augments and catalyzes the process rather than *distracting* you from it. You might not agree with any (or all) of what I present here. In fact, I might not agree with it myself down the road. You may think this is the stupidest stuff you've ever heard. (Actually, I'll probably look back and be amused by how trite and unevolved some of my statements were, as well.) If I've wronged you in the past, you might read this story and say "I knew it! She's out of her mind!" and you might be right.

But you might be wrong, too. That's part of *your* journey.

this is how I learned to roll

5/30/2010 (Sunday) – Prologue to the Experiment

If I disconnect from my virtual life, will I reconnect with my *REAL* one?

I've heard that admitting you *have* a problem is the first step towards *fixing* a problem. This is my confession. I am a social media addict. I did some data collection the other day and discovered just how bad my problem is. 1) I was checking Twitter (on average) every 8 minutes while awake. 2) I was checking Twitter nearly every 48 minutes while asleep. Since I sleep for eight hours a night, that translated into 10 Twitter checks *while asleep* and 120 checks a day *while awake*. But that's not the worst part, though! I have a Droid – a device I am completely in love with. But you know that little green light that blinks when an email, or a text message or a Google chat comes in? I was checking *that* about once every 2.5 minutes while awake. That's 384 adrenaline-loaded glances at my device a day, not counting the times I wake up in the middle of the night, which would definitely put me over 400. If each time represents a 5-second disruption to my life, that's:

400 Droid checks + 130 Twitter checks = 530 total checks x 5 seconds each = 2,650 seconds =

44.2 minutes a day OR

3% of my day

WASTED.

3

If I recover this 3%, how much more of my day — and my soul — will I recapture by figuring out something more satisfying to do with my mind, body and being? Doesn't sound like much, but I bet it will *feel* big.

I'd like to run this experiment for 6-8 weeks, but truthfully, that sounds like (and FEELS like) an eternity to me right now. So, the best I can do is to *take it one day at a time.*

I don't know what to expect from this experiment. I don't know if I'll even have the ability to get through it. To me, this is just as scary and impossible as trying to quit smoking when you're really enjoying it. I'm hoping I learn something useful about how to handle stress and anxiety a little better. I'm hoping I learn how to appreciate the things in my *real* environment a little more, and get new satisfaction out of those things. I want to get connected to the real world as pervasively as I've connected to the virtual world, and see if it improves my quality of life. Maybe I'll learn nothing, gain nothing, experience nothing.

But I think that's the fear talking, at least right now.

One day at a time.

Part I

Rules of Engagement

1.   I will not Tweet.

2.   I will not check Facebook (with the exception of direct messages, about once a week).

3.   I will not Google Chat with anyone. No Google Buzz either (this self-imposed restriction should be easy since I don't like Buzz at all).

4.   No Google Latitude! I do not need my mobile device to continually tell me *where I am* — I can look out the window. (This rule is subject to change if I am genuinely geographically *lost*.)

5.   I will disable the flashing green light on my Droid (hopefully this will eliminate the rush of adrenaline and endorphins stirred by the green flash, swiftly followed by the sinking feeling upon reading that all you got was a piece of spam).

6.   A few text messages a day is OK. (This includes direct messages from Twitter).

7.   Checking LinkedIn about once a week is OK.

8.   No updating my Google Chat status.

9.   I will check email and surf the net only at pre-designated times of day (TBD).

10.   No following blogs.

11.   No iGoogle.

Any of these rules can be waived in case of emergency.

(It will be interesting to see what I feel constitutes an emergency.)

5/31/2010 (Monday)

Today is the 4th day of *preparing* for technology detox. I have not checked Twitter since Saturday, meaning I've been "clean" for almost 48 hours. I haven't tweeted since Friday. That's 72 hours! I am about to bust out of my skin. What are my friends up to? What exciting news are they reading? What interesting studies are they sharing with their friends? Who's on a Memorial Day vacation this weekend, and where did they travel? Are they having fun? Am I having fun? If so, I've *got* to tell someone, right?

I just achieved one major accomplishment: I took a shower without my Droid. (No, I don't actually take the Droid *in* the water with me – then I'd be doing that rice bowl trick all the time, and jeopardizing the fabulous functionality of my device.) What I mean is that I typically place it on a towel outside the shower so that as soon as I get out, I can check for the flashing green light to see if anyone has tried to get in touch with me. The light rarely flashes for me but I never give up hope.

Tomorrow starts my "official" detox, which means I have to start following my own Rules of Engagement (with no cheating). I'm actually cheating a little bit right now – I have my Gmail window open on another tab (one that I'm not actively looking at) – so technically, I *can* see when a new email comes in because the number of unread messages will increase from 316 to 317. Also, I'm only "orange status" on Google Chat so any of my fellow Gmail friends could, conceivably, chat me—I'll see the "so and so says…" pop up on the Gmail tab. I'll tolerate none of that cheating tomorrow, though. I still feel myself looking at that darn

Gmail tab for new information every ten seconds or so – not healthy.

The stark truth that I have to face is that for the most part, no one wants to talk to me on a holiday weekend (online, that is). Everyone else has their own non-virtual life that they're probably living up pretty intensely right now. But not me – I'm sitting at my dining room table thinking about all the exciting things everyone else is doing, while I'm sitting at my computer *wondering what to do* with my life. Of course, if I was tweeting, *whatever I'd be telling you I was doing* would be exciting, too.

I need an outlet! I'm not going to make it through the whole summer without tweeting. If a tweet gets posted on Twitter, and no one really cares about it, does it matter? If a tweet gets thought, and never gets posted to Twitter, is the thought any less interesting or exciting?

Oh yay – a change on my screen – my Gmail tab now says 317! That means someone wants to get in touch with me. Instead of activating the Gmail tab, I'll check my email on my Droid to avoid Google Chat sadness – that is, seeing all the other people are online who don't want to chat. Oh, the adrenaline! I wonder what new email has arrived. (You may wonder why the tab says 317... confession: I have nearly 3000 emails in my Inbox, and over 300 are unread. I might have to deal with that at some point.)

So it's 2 seconds later, I responded to the adrenaline of the new email, and in full anti-climax I just deleted a new piece of spam. How dare they get my hopes up like that when all they want to do is sell me summer shoes on a holiday weekend?

Now, back to the matter at hand – I need an outlet. It can't be beer, because if I drink as much as I think about tweeting and checking social media online, I will *quickly* develop cirrhosis of the liver. My outlet can't be cigarettes, because even the hardiest of smokers only go through a pack or two a day. I would need more. Maybe exercise? Yeah, maybe. Or maybe "tweeting on paper". That's it! I'll just say whatever it is I was going to say on Twitter here in my journal. Seems sort of reminiscent of the older days – people writing their thoughts on paper, for no one to see, in paper journals. It's worth a shot. Remember: 140 characters or less.

> Remembering the severe consequences of a firmware error on the epidural pump 5 yr ago today. Happy bday Alex!
> 9:54AM on 5/31/2010 from paper-journal

Yes, today is my kid's birthday. And, actually, he's one of the reasons I'm doing this experiment. He wants his own Droid or Blackberry, and tentatively I've said OK, once he learns how to read. But I'd rather not get into a habit pattern where he's as addicted as I am, and we never do "normal" fun summer things like swimming or hiking. It's hard to hike peacefully when your Droid is out of signal and you need a fix! But I think the biggest disappointment of my tweetless policy right now is that other people don't get to know that it's Alex's 5th birthday. All of my tweets get automatically redirected to Facebook, so that means my Facebook friends won't get the message either.

Not that many of them – or any of them – would care anyway. The ones that would care will be calling today because they're family, and they want to wish him a happy birthday using the very personal and antiquated mechanism called the telephone.

I'm really surprised that I'm writing so much. The little voice in my head has a lot to say when it's not possessed by the habits of checking Twitter and Facebook. But I have to be honest too – I'm writing to keep my pen in my hand *and my Droid out of it.*

> Just disabled Google Chat. I'll miss you all. See you in 6-8
> weeks.
> 10:50AM on 5/31/2010 from paper-journal

Will anyone miss me? Probably not. You know, for years I had
this fantasy about just running away without a trace – starting a
new life – releasing myself from all the bonds (real and imagined)
of my fundamental existence. Now that I'm actually doing it, I'm
wistful, looking back over my shoulder as I drive out of town,
wondering if the decision to move away is one I'll regret.

> Made my hotel reservation at the T&C resort in San Diego
> for SPIE... yeah!
> 2:15PM on 5/31/2010 from paper-journal

Despite my net surfing, which very productively resulted in making this last reservation, I'm starting to feel a little more serene.
I disabled Google Chat and Google Buzz. *Now, no one can see
me* (I think) -kind of like in the olden days of the 1990's when
you were using a computer all by your lonesome self. Rather
refreshing!

> Subway sandwich + jalapenos + scharfer senf... holy
> smokes
> 5:29PM on 5/31/2010 from paper-journal

Aaagh! It's now only 5:50 PM and I caved. I tweeted for real,
using Twidroid on my Droid. Here's what I said: "Alex got a
chess board for his birthday, played his first game against me, and
WON fair and square." Well, maybe people will worry less when
I *stop* tweeting for real on June 1st, now that I've left this tiny
little digital breadcrumb.

Who am I fooling? No one is tracing my tweet frequency... no
one has been wondering how I'm doing... no one cares that I

just got the pants beat off me in chess, none the less by my son who technically won't be 5 years old for another three hours.

I'm as irrelevant to my virtual friends as they (pretty much) are to me. What a sad state of affairs, a full-moon lit dark night of the soul with rather little substance. I only tweeted once, for real, and I now I feel like a heroin addict who's indulged in the needle just one last time, for just one tiny little hit to get through the night.

> The unconscious holds the key to all of our life's desires. – something I heard on TV
> 10:01PM on 5/31/2010 from paper-journal

I'm not going to check my email tonight. I'm not going to get myself disappointed that no one wants to inquire about my whereabouts or wellness or well being. Power to the people! That is, to me :)

6/1/2010 (Tuesday)

It's the first day of hurricane season. Already there's a storm brewing within me, a disturbance in the Western Sahel of my psyche, but admittedly it's both a different shape and a different form from the one I was expecting. When I woke up to check my email this morning, I waited until 8:00 AM – the first accomplishment – and then found 7 messages in the Inbox. *None* of them were important, none of them were personal. Thanks to my heroic efforts disabling the addictive crack light on my Droid, the thing has not uttered the slightest flash since Saturday. I still throw glances at it throughout the day, half in disbelief, and half in vain and vapid anticipation. I have been psychologically conditioned to believe that there is redemption and renewal in that little flashing green light. Of course, neither redemption nor renewal is even embedded in the fantastic post-modern apps *within* the device. As a result, my implied expectations (however unreasonable) are slowly, daily, becoming raw and exposed.

GOAL: I will not check email until after noon, which is in 4 hours. I will scratch at least 2 items from my "to-do" list before I click "refresh" on my Inbox. (Side note: Obsessively checking email is really all I have now – except for checking Facebook direct messages, which I'm doing to do once every *other* day. That means today is my day "off" and so I must resist the beast. At least today's beast.)

I've heard that it only takes 21 days to establish a new behavior pattern, or to break the hardest part of an addiction. Part of me instinctively and intuitively recognizes the truth in this assertion. Two years ago, I was reeling from a terrible problem with insomnia. I hadn't really slept more than an hour or an hour and a half at a clip for the three years prior – a combined consequence of immersion in PhD school and new baby care – and I was on the brink of a very comfortable insanity. I yearned to disconnect then, but I had no idea *from what* I could disconnect. The pressures of day to day life were providing a panicked adrenaline. If I stopped moving, or thinking, or doing – *all of me* might stop, heart and soul included – and that I could not afford. So I turned to Ambien.

Ah, Ambien. I still have fond memories of my intimacy with you. You were like the skeleton key to a weathered old wooden door, holding on the other side an airy tropical resort, hammocks among the breezes, and blueness of sky and lapping waves. When I held you in my hand, escape was only 10 minutes away, and utter refreshment only 12 minutes away, for in your magic you eliminated the intervening 8 hours between the 10th and 12th minute. I did not care that you stole my hours. You provided me with far more reprieve than I'd get any other way, and so I grew to love you. Little did I know the days of our relationship were numbered.

21 days, in fact; that was the number. It was the sentence on my ephemeral fantasia, because when I went to the doctor to get a refill, his analysis was cold. "You're only 32. That stuff will rot your brain. I mean, I let my patients in their 50s and 60s do it, because in time their brains will rot pretty quickly anyway. But not you. You're headed to the sleep specialist."

I can't recount the story of our breakup right now, me and my Ambien, but I will later. Suffice it to say that 21 days later my life had changed, and only 17 days later my eyes had opened (making the final four days between 18 and 21 more bearable). I knew then that *there was a mystical merit in that two-digit number*, and from that point on I was a believer. At least a *casual* believer.

Sometimes it's hard to tell whether it's day 0... or day 4... or day 100.
9:01AM on 6/1/2010 from paper-journal

36 minutes until I can check my email again according to today's earlier goal.
11:24AM on 6/1/2010 from paper-journal

13 more minutes. Holding steady.
11:43AM on 6/1/2010 from paper-journal

While I'm waiting for "designated email checking time," I've just realized that I haven't looked at my Droid in about half an hour. *There will be nothing there,* I tell myself. No seductive flashing green light, no notifications, no promise of electronic adrenaline or dopamine, no excitement of "something better to do." Just a shiny black background where all I can see is my own reflection. *Maybe that's the point.*

The UVA campus is so beautiful and serene when all the students are gone for summer.
11:57AM on 6/1/2010 from paper-journal

Just walked 2.65 mi w/ @rduplain to Littlejohn's & back. All hail the Mushroom Melt.
1:47PM on 6/1/2010 from paper-journal

Just took a long walk through the UVA campus and told @rduplain all about my technology detox experiment. He wished me a lot of luck, and is confident I can learn some good things. When I inquired about whether he thought this was a good idea, the answer was pretty clear: "Yeah, you've been in pretty bad shape the past couple months."

The walk itself was pretty cathartic too. I realized a few things that I might want to remember, so I'll recount them here: 1) I'm really trying to figure out *who I am*. I've become too enmeshed in my virtual world to the point where it's hard to figure out *what I truly enjoy* anymore. 2) I'm trying to get beyond the feeling of "is this all there is to life?" and 3) I'm trying to focus on seeing and capturing emergent ("here and now") opportunities for fulfillment rather than living in the past – either previous fulfillment or *missed opportunities*. Classic mid-life crisis stuff, even though I'm still a little young for that.

Realization: I think nervous habits feed on nervous habits. In my heyday, the more I tweeted, the more I smoked. Of course, granted, there are caveats (known and unknown) which go beyond the scope of the present story. But maybe there's a detrimental positive feedback between these behaviors, each reinforcing the other until nerves and anxiety spiral out of control. Maybe like smoking, drinking, and coffee, stressful situations are all inexorably and intricately linked in the psyche of even the casual addict. (Someone should do some research into the traditional addictions, with "tweeting" thrown into the mix for comparison sake.)

Realization: I am an adrenaline junkie. The times I am the most "happy" are the times I am most excited by an idea, or person, or place, or thing. I put "happy" in quotation marks because I'm not sure that happiness is actually what I'm feeling. I may be (combining? convoluting? confounding?) happiness with the ability to focus on something for an extended period of time.

> First beep and green light from my Droid since Saturday.
> What can this be??? :)
> 2:22PM on 6/1/2010 from paper-journal

I can't believe how good that little "doink" noise from my Droid just made me feel. Two reasons: 1) I now have a REASON to look at my mobile device! and 2) there's probably someone who is genuinely interested in communicating with me.

Joy! It "doinked" again! Text message from Todd. That's what husbands must be for… convincing you that there's still some positive cheer associated with genuine communications of affection mediated by technology. His message to me? "Be careful at the hypnotist." So, yes, I'm headed to interview a hypnotist in just a few minutes. We'll see if that has any potential or utility for calming my busy mind.

Something caught my eye on the web and I'm kind of amazed, in light of my recognition earlier today that I'm an adrenaline junkie. This is from http://dictionary.reference.com/browse/twitter:

> twit · ter
> - verb (used without object)
> 1) to utter a succession of small, tremulous sounds, as a bird.
> 2) to talk lightly and rapidly, esp. of trivial matters; chatter.
> 3) to titter; giggle.
> 4) to tremble with excitement or the like; be in a flutter.

I think when they created the Twitter site, they were aspiring to definition #1. Somehow I've gotten ahead of them and moved all the way over to definition #4, and maybe even on to #5, which must be an allusion to a rip in the tapestry of mental fidelity.

> hi ho, hi ho, it's off to the dry cleaners and the hypnotist I go.
> 2:41PM on 6/1/2010 from paper-journal

Fast forward. It's 7pm, dinner has been eaten with the family, and I've only checked my Droid light once. I'm feeling a little calmer and a lot more insulated from the world – even picked up a *paper newspaper* today for some illumination! I've also got two books going – one by Ram Dass (the hippie guru psychologist from the 1970's) and then *Zen and the Art of Motorcycle*

Maintenance by Robert Pirsig. I have read both before, approximately 20 years ago. In fact, I think I've read each book multiple times since then, but I can't say I remember any of the story lines and I only have a vague sense of the messages. It is immaterial. I'm at a much different stage of my life, so these books will be new reading regardless. *The observer has changed and so the observed will similarly shift.*

I bet you're wondering what happened at the hypnotist today. But then again, the subconscious doesn't tweet, right?

> beat Alex at chess...barely. Kind of creepy how a new 5yr old nailed the rules in a day.
> 7:06PM on 6/1/2010 from paper-journal

6/2/2010 (Wednesday)

I mentioned yesterday that I'm reading a lot more – books, that is – now that I'm not fully betrothed to my computer and my Droid. I find it funny that regardless of the book I pick at the time I choose to read or re-read it, there's always a persistent message in the book for me (I added the emphasis here so you can see the part that's speaking to me):

> "What is happening in Western culture which is really awesome is that because of technology – not in spite of technology, because of technology – *the limits of our rational mind are becoming more apparent sooner.* And the limits of what take in terms of total fulfillment from the external world are becoming apparent earlier and earlier."
>
> Ram Dass, *The Only Dance There Is*, p. 148

To explain this point, Dass gives the example of how watching TV can actually benefit the evolution of individuality in kids. By watching so many programs, they are able to try out potential answers for the "what do you want to be when you grow up" question. Dass remarks that a 12 year old has probably vicariously tried on more than 200 roles and ideas – astronaut, lawyer, police chief, and so on – and by running through these experiences mentally, "he's gotten to the point where he is just here right now. He doesn't want to be anything. He's run out of them. He sees that all those aren't what it's going to be either."

I wonder if this is related to the vague feeling of discontent I've had for the past couple years – living vicariously, moving beyond the adrenaline of potential experiences (and in doing so, forgetting to stop and have my own experiences).

> "This is all out of technology, by the way. This is all out of the cultural philosophy of 'more is better'. We have collected more and more, and more and more, and the damning thing is that *more is never enough*."
>
> Ram Dass, *The Only Dance There Is*, p. 149

Keep in mind – this is from the transcription of a lecture given in 1970! They knew this stuff back then, even before I was born! *More is never enough.* And yet here I've been, opening up more and more and more and more receptors for incoming messages: email and Google Chat and Facebook, and Twitter direct messages, and Twitter regular messages, and oh yeah, the telephone too, and the U.S. Postal Mail. And *more is never enough*, because people will keep inventing more and more channels of communication. Soon, we will have no option but to forego many of them to at least favor, in part, the lower-bandwidth (yet more richly reverent) option of in-person conveyance of meaning. Or maybe telepathy will become commonplace, an option which will require even fewer bits (but at least we'll know that if a message actually gets through it was meant to be). I truly hope that the concept of "telepathic spam" is not feasible. But hold on – I forgot. That's been around us for decades already, and it's part of the problem of unwelcome randomness... it's called "advertising" or "marketing", or even "branding" – depending upon your motivations.

> been totally offline for over 12 hours. time to walk to Starbucks.
> 9:54AM on 6/2/2010 from paper-journal

> Walked 2.31 mi to Starbucks and back. What a beautiful day. Saw 18 goose-lings.
> 11:21AM on 6/2/2010 from paper-journal

I just spent a few minutes outside on my deck. It rained pretty profusely about a day and a half ago, and I noticed that there are little deposits of salt all over the wooden surface where the puddles evaporated. How can that be? Could the sky really have rained down all that salt, leaving such an obvious trace?

> "The subjective experience of doing something is that you confront some desire. A certain amount of wisdom makes you see that you aren't that desire. And wisdom starts to dislodge it just a little bit. Meditation, or bringing the mind to one point, dislodges it a little more because for moments you are free of it."
>
> Ram Dass, *The Only Dance There Is*, p. 165-166

Remarkable. I hadn't thought that this process of journaling my dis-attachment from the Internet and social technology could be a form of *meditation* — but it totally is! I've never been really patient with meditation, and in fact, have often rejected the practice as a waste of time (despite my rational mind's argument that so many *other* people can calm their mind this way, so why can't I?) Maybe meditation itself comes in various forms, like different styles of clothing; you have to find what *fits*.

> "Now, there are various strategies for how to work with a desire. One is not to do the things that the desire is connected with. Like my guru put a cup of tea in front of me, and said to me, 'Do you want it?' I'd say, 'Yeah.' He'd say, 'Then don't drink it.' Now, that's a very fierce strategy. See the predicament is that you might spend the next five hours wanting that cup of tea."
>
> Ram Dass, *The Only Dance There Is*, p. 166

Yep, that's my predicament. Can't have something, or decided that I'm going to "be strong" and not have it, and so I think about it for five hours. Or five days, or five weeks, or five

21

months. Hopefully not five years – that might be unbearable torture.

> "You can't not think of a rhinoceros the minute some-body tells you 'don't think about a Rhinoceros.' You can try to stop something prematurely, but in a way you are just feeding it. You are feeding the reality of it by the preoccupation. So the optimum strategy under those conditions seems to be to do whatever the things is, but remain as much as possible in the state of the *witness* – which in defense mechanism terms would be called dissociation. But it isn't dissociation out of anxi-ety. It's dissociation out of growth. So it isn't a defense mechanism."
>
> Ram Dass, *The Only Dance There Is*, p. 166

What I notice I have done is to attempt to deal with one desire by replacing it with another desire. I am journaling to take the place of an obsession with social media. I began my obsession with social media to replace the desire to *achieve*; you see, I'd been in PhD school for three years already, and the end of the struggle was in sight. I needed a replacement desire. I began to tweet and Facebook even more after I started my new life as a professor, in a defeated attempt to suppress the expansive desire to live as the free spirit I once was when I was a student in college. I have a neat and clean history of attempting to sup-press one desire by replacing it with another. (I can't believe not tweeting or checking social media for *less than a week* has led to this realization.)

> "There's the desire to achieve, or there's the desire for power, or there's that one running off. It's like a sublimi-nal flicker thing. You're doing something out of a desire that's taking you over, and then there's a moment when you see what you are doing.—which is usually followed by a judgmental moment. But then you witness the

22

judgment and you keep going through these little flickering things with the desires that you're not ready to stop because there's too much force in them still."
Ram Dass, *The Only Dance There Is*, p. 167

I guess it's normal that I felt like a heroin addict the other day when I tweeted after I said I wasn't gonna do it. My new response to the situation is detached. "Yep, I tweeted, and that's just what happened. Time to move on." There has just been too much force in my desires over the past several months, and that's what I'm working through. In fact, one of my first thoughts upon disconnecting was "What can I replace this habit with?" I was trying to trade one desire for another. This trading process could be an impassioned and dramatic infinite loop.

Did I mention I'm also re-reading that Pirsig book again? Here's a nice segment:

"When you've hit a really tough [problem], tried everything, racked your brain and nothing works, and you know that this time Nature has really decided to be difficult… you crank up the formal scientific method. For this you keep a lab notebook. Everything gets written down, formally, so that you know at all times where you are, where you've been where you're going, and where you want to get…otherwise the problem gets so complex you get lost in them and confused and forget what you know and what you didn't know and have to give up…sometimes just the act of writing down the problems straightens out your head as to what they really are."
Pirsig, *Zen and the Art of Motorcycle Maintenance*, p. 104-105

Clearly, this paper-journal is my lab notebook. I'm outlining in pretty elaborate detail where I am now and where I've been on this journey but there are three other things I need to think about. 1) Where am I? 2) Where am I going? 3) Where do I want to get to? And does that second question even matter?

have the strangest feeling that I'm in front of a vast treasure chest, and if only it wasn't invisible, I could open it.
1:08PM on 6/2/2010 from paper-journal

#firstwednesdays is at La Taza tonight! See you there.
2:16PM on 6/2/2010 from paper-journal

6/3/2010 (Thursday)

At 5:00am, the first bird makes its noise. Seconds later, several trees down from the first bird, another one responds – but it's hard to tell whether it's a true response, or just a noise that the second bird would have made on its own accord, whether or not the first one blazed the trail of sound. The pace picks up in a multitude of styles, each bird with its own tone and tempo in the almost distinguished bird-social-network where questions meet responses, and statements get restatements, and sometimes questions get questions and responses get nowhere. Before long the sounds are not individual, but collective, an oscillation between symphony and cacophony and back. In the online world, the early morning behavior is identical, only today I'm more aware of what's outside my windows than what you can get to through Windows. If there was a way to "visualize" the morning mass arrival of people's ideas in to the virtual realm, with sounds, would it be more of a *symphony* or more of a twisted, mangled mess?

> Had a great time at #firstwednesdays. La Taza is an excellent summer venue! Thx @cloudbrain
> 9:02AM on 6/3/2010 from paper-journal

First Wednesdays is a gathering of technology professionals that takes place (this should not be surprising) on the first Wednesday of each month. About 10am in the morning on that first Wednesday of the month, the "secret location" of the gathering is tweeted and retweeted throughout Charlottesville. About 20 to 30 of my Twitter connections show up at each event, so when I attended the gathering this time, I felt strangely (and almost virtually) connected again. It's a really enjoyable time, and typically involves more than enough beer and conversation. Some people noticed that I hadn't been online – that was nice. Everyone asked what project I was working on this summer, so I had the opportunity to share Project Disconnected and get some feedback.

The response was surprising! Most people initially responded with a "wow, I'd like to do that / I've thought of doing that / I should do that." There were a couple people who said "I could never do that," and a handful of "yeah, I tried that" responses. The people who *had* tried to disconnect, though, had only claimed a few days or couple weeks offline – and that was when they were on vacation. When I mentioned that I was journaling the whole experience, one guy said, "wow, you're like wirelessly blogging and microblogging at the same time! Are you gonna put that on the web? I could follow it." I was really honored by the enthusiasm of that response, but I think the *point* is that my reflections are not immediately publicly consumable.

I really did have a great time, though. Rather than remain connected to my wider virtual world, I was able to concentrate my mental, emotional, and "fun" energy and really have some intense and bizarre conversations. Illuminating. I think, in my social connectedness through the virtual world, that somehow I had become more emotionally invested in what other people were doing, which fragmented my Self on a daily basis. Here's what I mean: if I was following 100 friends, and they were scattered all over the globe doing interesting things, a part of me would be present *with them,* vicariously enjoying the energy of those experiences in those 100 places. From tapping into all those experiences, I would become part of those experiences, and with a tiny part of me at each one *I could be everywhere* at one moment in time.

But the more of *everywhere* you are part of, the more that *everywhere* gradually becomes *nowhere*. What happens after that is that you realize the whole concept of *here* has become lost in the process too, and you don't remember how to get back *there* either.

> Instead of reading @dailyprogress I'm actually reading The Daily Progress (on paper). Neat.
> 9:29AM on 6/3/2010 from paper-journal

There's a lot more to the newspaper, I'm finding out, than the stories that are tweeted online by Matt (aka @dailyprogress). Before this week, I saw no need for the newspaper on paper. But now that I'm offline, I'm getting some sort of kinesthetic satisfaction from browsing through the hidden stories that would never make the ranks of the 140-character marquis. For example: I have never seen an obituary tweeted, even though sometimes it's curious to browse through that section of the newspaper, even if it's just to get a glance of who's moving on and where they've been, even if their stories are *ordinary*.

Realization: Social media feeds can help you find the interesting or noteworthy stories, but not the *ordinary* stories. And the ordinary stories are just as much a part of life, and maybe even more so.

> "I feel happy to be here, and still a little sad to be here too. Sometimes it's a little better to travel than to arrive."
>
> Pirsig, *Zen and the Art of Motorcycle Maintenance*, p. 116

When I'm not traveling – that is, moving towards a goal or just to another place on the Earth's surface – I feel like I've already arrived somewhere. Some wellspring deep within me has the energy of a shark who's just got to keep moving, and in the absence of motion, the shark blood sputters and boils at rest. But tweeting and facebooking and chatting can give you the impression that you're sharking around the waters, swiftly twisting and moving somewhere fast, when in fact, you've never left your seat. Maybe that's why I was so attracted to it.

"That's how I roll." I've heard this statement, on average, at least once every three days for the past month or so. It must be showing up in my world because I need to think about it more. I heard the phrase – overheard it actually – again last night, from some guy behind me at #firstwednesdays: "that's how I roll, you know?" The little voice in my head was emphatic: "No! I don't actually know." Rolling is such a passive activity, one that is not predisposed to interacting or relating with other people or other things. But beyond this recognition, it became apparent to me that *I don't really know how I roll*. Other people have clearly gained some contentment in knowing how *they* roll, which to me should shed some light on the questions of "who am I," "where am I," and "why does it matter." It can't be coincidence that this phrase is poking itself into my life so unabashedly as of late, uninvited.

> So fun when you think you have free time and then recall a 1pm meeting 15 mins away by car. Groan…
> 12:15PM on 6/3/2010 from paper-journal

> Fish tacos at Bel Rio…five thumbs up
> 7:44PM on 6/3/2010 from paper-journal

There's a survey on the front page of today's USA Today that asks "what is the only thing you can't live without?" 41% said having an intimate relationship. 40% said *my smartphone*. 17% said morning coffee. 3% said checking social network sites. Of course, it's all context and situation dependent… but today, I'd have to say I'm in the 40%.

I just set my Google Latitude location to Boulder, Colorado. I am not in Boulder, but I've been thinking about going back there for a while. I've also been thinking about how so many people I've talked to find it easy to – or easier to – live in the moment when they are not in their ordinary environments. So for the time being, my soul is going to be stationed in Boulder, and I will drink the majesty of the Flatirons and the downtown jazz clubs and the radiant, thin air as I pursue consciousness and awareness. If Google Latitude says I'm in Colorado, where else could I possibly be? So here I go: to Colorado, in my mind and on my Droid.

But my body is in Charlottesville, Virginia, and that's fine with me tonight. Because the fish tacos I had tonight were local, and not from Wahoo's, and the thunderstorms have been right in my backyard. Today, at least, there is no better place to stomp around in the puddles in bare feet and listen to the lovely rumbling of the rain and hail and thunder all packaged in one night's comfort.

I'm loving tonight's thunderstorms even though they're not severe @traviskoshko @cbs19weather
8:55PM on 6/3/2010 from paper-journal

6/4/2010 (Friday)

It just dawned on me that there is something I need to explain. I *do not* feel as if my nervous habit of checking emails and Google Chat and Twitter and Facebook is the real, underlying problem. What I recognize is that this nervous habit has been obscuring other problems that I need to uncover and deal with. The ultimate joke may be on me. At this point, I have no idea what those problems might be, let alone the solutions. I'm my own patient, presenting symptoms that are nebulous and shifting and indicative of the first case of its kind. I am suspended between the planes of technology and spirituality, desperately seeking an edge.

> busy day: chiropractor, observatory, endocrinologist, hypnotist.
> 8:21AM on 6/4/2010 from paper-journal

> CNN just noted that "Forrest Gump was always in the right place at the right time." Me too.
> 12:08PM on 6/4/2010 from paper-journal

Right now, my body is at the endocrinologist's office. I feel like I was just here, but I think the last real time I was here was 18 months ago. Usually, I'd be sitting in a doctor's waiting room tweeting and facebooking – clearly, other people are doing way more fun things right now and I want to be where they are rather than where I am. And traditionally, my Droid would help me get there. Today is a little different though, and at this point I'm just trying to think about whatever it is I'm thinking about, and relax into being me for a few moments.

So what I'm thinking about is actually a tagline created by my friend Valdis Krebs, who analyzes all kinds of networks (including social networks). What he says (and what I'm thinking about right now) is "connect on your similarities, profit from your differences." I think it's much easier online to connect with other people based on the similarities you have with them – and much easier to focus on the differences you have with people you are around in the real world. Think about work environments, and how they naturally socially stratify into people you really like being around, people you feel neutral towards, or people you feel completely alienated from. That third group of people is much easier to identify in person because they are less easily ignored; people you don't like will capture your attention, typically in ways you don't like. People you like are easily identified if you're continually sharing interests, and that's very easily done online. As with all other observations in this journal though, I might be wrong too.

The other thing I'm thinking about is how my right ear has been completely unclogged since I went to the chiropractor this morning. When your bones are out of balance, wow, those guys can be miracle workers. My ear has been bugging me for a couple of months. Should I tweet about that? Nahhh... not interesting enough for my 3rd tweet of the day. And tweets have *got* to capture interest.

> waiting in dr's office... STILL... re-read the March 2010 Reader's Digest that I read on another dr. visit
> 12:50PM on 6/4/2010 from paper-journal

There was actually one pretty funny thing on the last page of that March 2010 Reader's Digest. It was a Venn diagram that looked kind of like this:

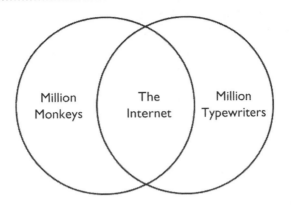

Getting healthy in the psyche, and developing a positive, non-codependent relationship with technology (and in particular, social media), is enhanced by a sound body. Starting Monday, my body will be getting sounder. My endocrinologist, amused by the total absence of reflexes in my elbows that he observed during our meeting this morning, is giving me more of his kind of secret medicine to close the gaps. I give my total support.

> what would happen if you hypnotized yourself before an appt w your hypnotist? wd they notice?
> 1:38PM on 6/4/2010 from paper-journal

"Maybe if your creativity had fewer outlets, it would come out of you with more force."

Cartoon in *The New Yorker,* Dec 21 & 28, 2009, p. 128

In the process of plugging up so many of my technologically driven leaks, I'm finding that there's a little more of a concentrated outlet for me to enjoy and be present in each day and in each moment.

> The hypnotist says that I'm really intrigued by "dark night of the soul" experiences
> 4:39PM on 6/4/2010 from paper-journal

33

6/5/2010 (Saturday)

I watched TV last night and then fell asleep for 11 hours. That turn of events is *definitely* not interesting enough to be tweetable. Then I woke up this morning, rushed to check email, and found one piece of spam which I promptly deleted. I'm noticing a trend here. *There's really very little content of importance that's been flowing in.* Now granted, it's summer, and I'm not teaching again until August. I recognize that a slow flow of incoming requests for your attention is a luxury many people do not have. In fact, I've planned this summer to have little action or excitement, and although I spent much of May regretting that decision, I think spending time with myself and my reflections is something that needs to be done.

After my two minutes of entirely emotionally unsatisfactory spam deletion, I read the Daily Progress on paper. Me and my coffee indulged in the whole newspaper, sitting in the kitchen at the island, feeling the morning breeze – the breeze that will soon either stop (or become unbearable) as we are confronted once again with today's 95 degree reminder that our air conditioning is broken and won't be fixed until at least Monday.

I am not one who likes the cold. In fact, it's my contention that even in Virginia, winter continues through May and resumes promptly in September. I yearn for the days of 80's and 90's and even higher, but now that I totally have what I "want", I'm starting to appreciate the relief that a climate controlled interior would bring.

> some days, I just feel like I have nothing useful to tweet.
> 10:07AM on 6/5/2010 from paper-journal

Even through no one is reading my tweet journal, I still feel remarkably self-conscious about what I am paper-tweeting. I want to give the impression that I'm engaged and having fun with something, even though I'm just sitting at my dining room table with no energy to do anything today.

It's not like I don't have anything to do: I could finish that SPIE conference paper that was due last week. I could vacuum up the baking soda I scattered on the carpet two days ago. I could make my reservations to get to San Diego and back. I could clean out my cluttery car. I could send one simple email asking members of my ASQ Software Division group (a professional society) to submit newsletter articles. I could do laundry. I could go to the Farmer's Market. I could take a shower. I could return that miserable laptop to the store, the one that has the impossible mouse pad design, the one that we're never going to be able to use with a positive attitude. I could write a grocery list, and go to the store and get the groceries. This last one is fairly important; we are running out of everything, even the staples like milk and water.

But to me, each of these options sounds as dull and uninteresting as the others. Before my excuse for not doing them was that I had too much "work" to do online, and maybe I did. Now I have no excuse because I am not online, and the foundation of my argument crumbles to reveal the emptiness underneath.

Realization: Obsessively following the "buzz" online has been keeping me from truly spending time with myself. It's gotten in the way of finding balance... and cultivating a sense of peace so I have the energy to go out into the world, and maybe get those much needed groceries.

Self-disgust has grabbed me by the arm and shaken the vacuum loose from its hideaway. The Arm & Hammer has been sucked up and is now resident in the vacuum bag. The floor has been happily Pine-Sol'd out of anger, the trash has been pushed off the table. Where is my *motivation*? I'm offline and I can't *accomplish* anything without getting disgusted at myself... at least so far today!

I've been thinking a lot about motivation, probably because I seem to have so little of it. Funny how *lacking* something totally makes it something you think about *all the time*. When I was still in school *lacking* a PhD but desperately trying to get one, I thought about the process and the outcome constantly. When I couldn't sleep, in the depths of my raging insomnia, all I thought about was the bliss of unconsciously free-floating through space. When you're hungry (especially when you want to lose weight) all you can think of is food. When you have no friends, you ponder the concept a lot. When online Texas Hold 'Em payoffs were outlawed, I twitched at the prospect of no more payout on the flop, turn and river.

In any case, *motivation*. Epitomizing my struggle is the story of *Drive*. That is, I bought Daniel Pink's book called *Drive: The Surprising Truth about What Motivates Us* a few months ago. It seems like an interesting read, but I just haven't been able to pick it up off the back seat of my car, where it's been sitting ever since it left its original nest at the bookstore. Yeah, motivation – what drives us? More importantly, what drives me, and how can I get it *back*? We'll have to think about this a little more. Put the thought on the back burner. The book can stay on the back seat a little longer.

> Misread the label as "insatiable tape". If it really was, you'd have to use the whole roll, and maybe more.
> 12:22PM on 6/5/2010 from paper-journal

That makes sense. *If a desire really is insatiable,* you should just stop now and save the world a whole lot of adhesive tape.

There's a word that starts with a "C" that I've been racking my brain about lately. I can't for the life of me remember it. It's an important word... means "you're mashing two concepts together in a completely inappropriate way and it's confusing your thoughts." Not confusing, co-mingling, confessing, composting, conflagrating, confounding... but oh, the process of trying to figure this word out is indeed confounding.

Jupiter and Uranus are going to be hanging out with one another in the sky over the next five months. I'm going to have to find an optical telescope and check them out. I was surfing a bit online to find out more about it and found this neat little gem that resonates with me:

> "Love delivers truth with wisdom, honesty, grace and clarity. Truth on its own can come out a bit sharp and forceful. Practice this in daily life. When you have to say something, say it with love and all the other qualities."
>
> celestialspace.wordpress.com

I appreciate truth, but I also think it has to be delivered in such a way that the person who receives the message can grow rather than die, as a result. I'm sort of using the same approach as I talk myself through this journal.

I've found myself spending quite a bit of time deleting and archiving messages from my Gmail account. I don't consider it time spent totally online, because I have Google Buzz and Google Chat turned off until further notice, and I'm finding out no one really sends me anything anyway – so it's as if I'm not connected at all. Sort of (OK, so I'm stretching it). But I am deleting old baggage... started at almost 3,000 messages in the Inbox, and

I'm now down to 2,244. Maybe I'll get them all handled before the end of the summer, but I'm not going to pressure myself.

There's a guy named Merlin Mann who believes that the secret to reclaiming your life and your attention is to get all the junk out of your Inbox, thus achieving the Zen state of "Inbox Zero". He has an expansive collection of tips and tricks for getting to this state and keeping your Inbox clean so you don't have to "live there". It sounds like a good idea, although I don't know if I'd really be committed enough to consistently apply the tips and tricks. But there are a few concrete steps I've taken that he espouses: 1) I got off of all the email lists that I was archiving but never reading, 2) I started deleting old emails that "I might need someday", and 3) I transcribed phone numbers OUT of old emails and into my phone records. It's a start.

Realization: To live a meaningful life, you have to minimize the amount of time you spend doing soul-less, value-less activities. Even "biding your time" is rather vacuous.

> If I don't go to the grocery store now, we'll all starve to death.
> 3:50PM on 6/5/2010 from paper-journal

6/6/2010 (Sunday)

Last night was a very quiet evening. I was tired of thinking, tired of talking, tired of getting check-mated by my 5 year old again... but mostly tired out thanks to my utter lack of Saturday accomplishments. I'm still glancing at my Droid multiple times a day even though rationally, I know that since I've shut the light off, it's rather unlikely for it to blink (and if it does, I may want to consider exorcism). I've also not heard that enticing little "doink" noise for days, other than in my sleep.

A few months ago I was at a bar with some friends when I hastily confessed that I checked Twitter in my sleep. (I didn't think this was a problem... I thought everyone else checked Twitter in their dreams too). It had become such a natural part of my dream life that I was to the point where I could even tell people who *weren't* on Twitter what their userids were in my "dream Twitter space".

In retrospect, I probably should have considered this a sign of needed change. But like I said, I didn't even think of it as weird, and in fact when the topic was first raised, I was pretty surprised that my technology infused friends didn't tweet in *their* dreams too.

I have now wasted about half an hour "somewhat surfing" the net and putting off my morning walk to Starbucks. It's getting hotter every minute. Time for some prioritization.

> Off on a morning walk to Starbucks and to see those 18 excellent geese lings
> 9:04AM on 6/6/2010 from paper-journal

41

> 2.65 mi and a line out the door…we will have D&D coffee at home this AM
> 10:12AM on 6/6/2010 from paper-journal

One of the things I appreciate when I go on these walks is that *I'm by myself.* There is no need for conversation, even though the little voice in my head is very lively in dialog with me nearly the whole time. We have no expectations of each other, though, so the conversation always flows naturally, and when it stops, there is no pressure for more. We'll both return to cultivating our close relationship when the time is right, and so there's no pressure for progress either. We are not threatened by long-term separations that are precipitated by "busy-ness" – we know there will be many more conversations in the future.

Walking is very meditative. You get in the flow of putting one foot in front of the other, and then the scenery changes a little bit, and then you just do it again. I remember not too long ago I was talking to my friend Jordan, who manages a bank. She has a 5 year old boy just like me, but also has a 3 year old girl, so I'd say she's much busier than I am. We got talking about meditation and all these "benefits" we hear that meditation can bring. Oh, how we would love to be that peaceful, and relaxed, and balanced! *If only we had the time.* "I would totally meditate if I could multitask and do it while I was getting something else done… like driving!" she said. I agreed.

So I'm walking this morning, and me and the little voice are having a very flowing conversation, and then it hit me: *I am actually meditating right now.* I have detached from the rest of the world, I am indulging in solitude, and my only goal is to keep one foot in front of the other and keep moving forward. Eventually, I will get somewhere. But the goal isn't really to get there, it's just to keep moving, stay in the flow, and give the little voice some air time. It never gets a chance to really expound on a topic unless I spend a little time alone and in the quiet. I wonder if, when you have tension in your life, that tension is just the reflection of

a frustrated little voice, who's saying "no one ever listens to me, and I have all this useful commentary to offer.
Why bother?"

I think meditation is "sold" the wrong way. It's not something that requires bowls of water, or wafting nag champa, or lots of soothing Sanskrit incantations. It's not even religious at all, which is something that had me confused for many years. (Although if all that ritualistic stuff works for you, by all means go for it.) When I'm walking in the quiet of the mid-morning (I'm not an early bird), I am definitely in a meditative state. How do I know? Because the little voice in my head is happy, and active, and content, and engaged.

Unreal. I just heard my Droid "doink" again, as clear as the sirens outside. There are no messages. It was an auditory hallucination.

OK – so, meditation. That's where we were. If I can intensely (and effortlessly) meditate while on a long walk, that's definitely multitasking, right? Imagine how many more people would meditate if the whole practice was framed differently. "Lose weight...meditate!" Two or three miles a day, think about your goals for just today, then embark on your day and get a few things done. Imagine if you surveyed a group of frazzled moms, or stressed-out managers, or teachers (especially preschool teachers who, in my opinion have nerves of steel). Ask them two questions: 1) Would you like time to meditate? 2) Would you like time to spend in solitude with just yourself and the quiet, escaping from all the noise of the world, and maybe getting a chance to totally relax?

I think there would be a lot of "no" answers on #1, and a lot of "Hell, yeah!" answers on #2. Both questions are asking the same thing. See, it's all a part of the packaging. I would have actually started "meditating" a long time ago if I thought it would be a respite from the chatter of my household and my workplace.

Or if someone told me "just imagine you're going on vacation... only it's one hour at a time, in little pieces, scattered throughout your month." Yeah, I might have done that.

To get back to my house, the last part of the walk is uphill. Walking uphill is less fun than walking downhill, but ultimately more instructive. When you're walking uphill, and you're tired and sweaty and it's getting hotter minute by minute, frustration sets in pretty well. Some people who walk or run a lot might enjoy this state of being, but not me. (I'm more sedentary than those athletes because I've spent so much time with my computer over the past couple decades, but don't get me wrong, it's not like I'm totally out of shape or anything). My frustration this morning took the form of questioning *why in the world* did I ever set out on a walk on such a hot morning. Grrrr. I should have envisioned this miserable return trip uphill to get home. This sucks.

That's when the "meditative groove" kicked in and my little voice decided to share its wisdom. "Nothing you can do will make the distance to your house shorter...or longer. There's just a span of time, here and now to then, that you're going to have to lumber through – and that's just the way it is. So stop wasting your energy getting frustrated, and just keep putting one foot in front of the other, and that's that." OK, little voice, gotcha. I don't have any better advice for myself. But isn't it *all* like that? Everything you go through in life occurs over a span of time. That span of time is going to have a certain shortness or a certain longness, but that's all. Much of the time you're not going to be able to change it, so you just have to flow through it. And that's always going to be easier when you don't tense your body up. Like for example: think about the last time you were unhappy, or mad, or grieving. Chances are, you were part of that feeling for a while, then you flowed right out of it into a differ-ent feeling. The emotion had its own shortness or longness, and rather than getting frustrated by trying to influence the feeling, you could have just rolled with it.

44

A ha!! There's that mysterious phrase again! Maybe that's the key... rolling and flowing and "enjoying the journey"... maybe those concepts all refer to the same thing. Accepting that every feeling and experience has its own shortness or longness, but that *your* job is just to keep the feet moving in whatever sustainable way you can. Home is always at the top of the hill.

> still stressed about not having my SPIE pprs done. A week late now.
> 11:32AM on 6/6/2010 from paper-journal

I'm starting to see that all of my tweets have an ulterior message, a hidden subtext that is probably meant to convey to my social network that I have a certain personality characteristic. This one said "Hey! I've got to be working and productive on a Sunday!" The last one said "Hey! I'm trying to be industrious on a Sunday morning by taking a long walk!" I wonder if all tweets, pulled from the collective unconscious of all possible tweets, are so selectively chosen or accidentally (subconsciously) censored, like mine.

I can't retweet from here, on paper. I feel like I'm not fulfilling the important trivial social responsibility of passing along the Hot Potato of Seemingly Useful Digital Information. I have no virtual hands right now; can't handle any potatoes at all in that world.

It's been a week now that I haven't checked (or done) Twitter or Facebook or Google Chat statuses. You can't see or hear me. And I'm choosing not to see or hear you, whether you know it or not.

> "Be a provenance of something gathered, a summation of previous intuitions, let your vulnerabilities walking on the cracked sliding limestone be, this time, not a weakness but a faculty for what's about to happen."
> David Whyte, *The Seven Streams*

45

The pool is a beautiful space to spend a 92-degree afternoon & 1.2 mi walk.
3:09PM on 6/6/2010 from paper-journal

I haven't cooked that much in the past few years, and I'm sure part
of the reason is that you *can't cook when you're online too much.*
Tonight I grilled baby bok choy. Cut it in half lengthwise, doused it
in an equal mixture of sesame oil, lemon juice, and soy sauce, and
popped it on the charcoal grill for about 5 minutes. Afterwards,
I drenched it in an equal mixture of horseradish, mayonnaise, and
water. That part is optional. I am impressed that such an invention
emerged from my non-online self. You should try it! (Ordinarily,
this is the kind of thing I would post on a Facebook Note. Not
today, or this week, or 'til I finish Project Disconnected.)

I was told that when you're going through major transitions in
life, which I'm sure my experience right now will be part of (although I'm also sure I won't actually understand *how* this was a
life transition until years later) – you should record your dreams.
Sometimes, it's the little voice inside your head telling you things
in the form of pictures and movies rather than plain prose.

My last night's dream may have some clues, but it seems simultaneously trivial and obfuscatedly significant. I was in my office,
next to a conference room where horizontal tables that could
seat two or three were aligned in two rows with an aisle down
the middle. There were three rows of two tables each, wooden-
looking Formica on top, in a dimly lit room. It was almost as
if someone was about to start a PowerPoint presentation, but
no one was there except for one guy I work with sitting at the
front table. Even though this was supposedly a familiar place, of
course in the world of dreams, everything felt brilliantly familiar
but it was completely unlike anything resembling my *real* office.

I had gone outside to my car; the car in my dreams. (Not *of*
my dreams, as you'll see.) It was "new," purchased for me only

a few days earlier by my husband, but clearly not a new car
and more clearly not my style. It was like a 1930's version of
a VW beetle, the peach color of contented flesh and apricots,
only with a slightly disturbing feature: it looked like it had been
hand-painted with a brush. I was not very enthusiastic about his
choice for me in cars. It seemed far too removed from my actual
needs, as if he didn't even know what kind of car I might like, despite years of data observing the things that I like and don't like.
There were artificial purple wisteria in a flower-box across the
whole front dash though, and those were kind of nice.

I got to my car, this new and completely mismatched thing, with
no keys – so I headed back inside. There were no keys in my
office either, so the next stop was the dimly lit conference room,
just as stagnant and waiting for me as it was before, the blue
screen anticipating *something*.

My keys and wallet were on the front table on the right, so I
went to pick them up. My friend looked aloof, tired, almost
bored in his seat, head in hand. With a tone that was just a tiny
bit edgy and impatient, he said, "I knew you'd have to come back
some time. You left your keys and wallet." In real life, though,
he would have been commenting on his surprise that I'd left my
Droid behind, a scenario that's played out once or twice in real
life.

The weekend has been sluggish and nearly backwards, like a
vague joke I remember about Mississippi. Tomorrow will be different. So far, the past couple days have just felt rather vacant
and tweetless.

6/7/2010 (Monday)

Chess and cooking are also rather meditative activities. Chess, because if I don't immerse myself in the moment, I'm going to get to beat by my 5 year old son. (Can't believe he's only been playing the game for a week.) Cooking, because when it's just you and the mushrooms or onions or peppers and the knife, it's important to get in the zone so you don't lose a finger. I must have gotten in a good space this morning because I checkmated my kid in only 20 minutes.

> A/C man is on his way…figures, it's 15 deg cooler than it's been in 2 weeks.
> 9:12AM on 6/7/2010 from paper-journal

It's not frighteningly apparent why I've been so unmotivated the past few days, and unmotivated in particular to finish writing that conference paper. It's on decision analysis for software acquisition based on lifecycle costing (maybe that's the problem). Writing the paper is just *not* the most authentic activity I could be doing right now. Where is my soul? Well, my soul is pretty happy indulging in all of this reflection, writing page after page of the winds that are flowing through me, sorting and twisting and rearranging all the information and intuition that's clogged me for months now (if not years). I've written 19 pages over the past few days, which is a little over 3,000 words of reflection. A typical academic journal paper in my discipline is about that long… in fact, the one I finished on May 31st was 3,486 words, and that counts my name and address and all those auxiliary words that don't ever contribute to the message.

Two days ago, if anyone had told me "go write a 3,000 word reflection" on any topic, I would have laughed at the prospect. Come on! I've got writer's block! I can't come up with 3,000 words. But that's precisely what I've done, *effortlessly*, by spending my time on the most authentic activity I can possibly be doing right now.

Wow! That's, like, the recipe for a perpetual motion machine. Limitless energy. Something out of nothing.

Over the past two decades I've studied a lot of physics, and even got myself a degree in meteorology, which is basically a physics degree only that you focus on the most relevant physics and ignore all the rest. But I've always had a deep psychological discontent with the whole "conservation of energy" thing. That's the law that says if a system is isolated (that is, doesn't interact with its surroundings), the total amount of energy in it will remain constant over time. It's also the law that says energy can't be created or destroyed; it only changes from one state of being into another.

Ideas are the reason I have a problem with the whole conservation of energy thing. (Now don't get me wrong – I've seen tons of examples within the physical world that clearly establish a role for conservation of energy and that it's a physical truth in the sense that's been very useful in developing in our understanding of nature.) I just don't see energy being conserved as ideas emerge and make their ways into the world.

Imagine a trade show, or a big meeting or conference, in a conference center. There are rooms of all sizes to fit sessions with 10 attendees, 100 attendees, maybe even 1,000 attendees. A speaker gets up and delivers the same message to each audience in each room. No one has ever heard the message before, and it's delivered in the same way and at the same time with the same intonation and gestures. Everyone is uniformly inspired, and leaves the session equally as energized as everyone else. If there is energy in the delivery of the message, and even considering that the idea itself may have some inherent energy, what just happened in each of those three conference rooms? We can't expect that the energy of the message was divided among the participants, otherwise the folks in the 1,000-person session would really have lost out, leaving with only 1/1000 of the original energy of the idea. The folks in the room of 10 would be leaving with 1/10 the energy of the presentation, a whole bunch compared to those other attendees.

But we can't even say that the energy is divided and distributed, because the person *delivering* the message hasn't *given any of it away* for good. It's still there inside him or inside her, and hasn't *lost* any energy at all. In fact, the one who delivered the message may be themselves energized by the interaction with the audience, making even more energy!

Inspiration does not seem to follow the principle of conservation of energy. We can make some of it from nothing. We can inspire one person with the same amount of energy it takes to inspire millions! The energy can be lossless! Infinite! Immortal!

For years, when this idea crossed my mind, I was convinced that the excess energy had to come from food. Or maybe our cells and those wonderfully energetic reserve molecules we can draw from inside ourselves. But it just doesn't seem to equate to the energetics of the kind of inspiration that can lead people to do great things. Or even not-great things, like getting the energy to do laundry or go to the grocery store. You might laugh. Do I really need to be inspired to get off my butt and go to the store to get food? Yeah, actually I confess that I do. I am not one of those people on autopilot, dutifully attending to their to-do list and going through the motions. I am not satisfied by "just going through the motions" without utter authenticity. I have a hard time dealing with the ordinary to-do's of daily life.

And yet I still deal with obsessive and compulsive behaviors where technology is concerned, or at least the ghost or remembrance of them, locked up in a coma now for just over a week. It all seems so weak and vulnerable, and having considered myself a strong person, I'm also embarrassed that this topic has such a hold over me at the moment. (The same goes for any other topic or subject or object that's yielded the same internal dynamics. They are all the same.)

> this is a secret message
> 11:43AM on 6/7/2010 from paper-journal

Emotional anchors are funny, and mostly non-sequitur. We grilled some pork ribs last night and I'm cutting up some cold leftovers for lunch today. I take a cold bite and I'm camping in Death Valley somewhere at 2 or 3,000 ft as the early morning sun hints at the burnt topaz and bronze below. I'm breathing the chill of the desert and the rocks because I can't find my shoes.

> "The 19th century German philosopher Arthur Schopenhauer held that even the best life possible for humans is one in which we strive for ends that once achieved, bring only fleeting satisfaction. New desires then lead us on to further futile struggle and the cycle repeats itself."

Peter Singer in "Should this be the last Generation?", *New York Times*, 6/6/2010

Cutting zucchini is also very meditative. You have 6 zucchini in front of you and your job is to slice. Slice, slice, slice until it becomes a rhythm beyond yourself, even though you're the slicer.

> fixin to take a walk to see those 18 baby geese. little 747s on test flights.
> 6:38PM on 6/7/2010 from paper-journal

Slice, slice, slice. After I got through the zucchini I decided to apply the same technique to my oh-so-late conference paper. I need 8 pages, and each of them is now 8 days late. Three slices later I have two pages done and a lot more confidence. Maybe that's the ticket. Now, just gotta keep on slicing, little bit at a time.

Realization: You need a slick pen with a lot of good ink to keep up the motivation to write in a journal. Time to switch pens.

I haven't checked Facebook in over a week and quite frankly, it's eating me alive. What's everyone up to? It's summer! Want to get together? Don't know! I can't live vicariously through your experiences if I can't look them up... and so I'm forced to look for my own.

We're now on official Day 8. With my other extrication experience, my eyes had opened by Day 17. That means here are only 9 days until I can recount that transitional tale. In the meantime, I've identified my proxies for checking Twitter and Facebook so much:

1) I check for earthquakes at quake.usgs.gov
2) I check the national radar for storms & tornadoes
3) I've been living in my Inbox a little too excessively, waiting for the Nothing that invariably shows up.
4) I'm deleting and archiving the messages in my Gmail Inbox. Started around 3,000 – down to about 1,500. (Funny what productivity nervous tension can yield.)

A nice, cool evening to cover 1.6 mi, but only 3 little geeselings
8:25PM on 6/7/2010 from paper-journal

There are 4 deer right behind my car attm, which is parked in the driveway
8:46PM on 6/7/2010 from paper-journal

6/8/2010 (Tuesday)

Slice, slice, slice. I'm still lacking the energy to work on my conference paper, but finding that I'm fully capable of *effortlessly* attacking another slice of the problem as long as the slice is thin enough. Thin slices are also interesting defenses against getting interrupted... it's much easier to interlace chess games and toasting toast and getting Alex his milk and listening to him talk about his racecars and making progress on my still-oh-so-late paper when the slices are thin.

In between slices, though, I'm still stagnant at my dining room table, slightly vacuous and totally empty. I'm keeping my psyche out of my Inbox today, and with no new books to read to navigate my reflection, I might have to start reading books backwards again. First chapter, last chapter, then [chapter last minus one] through [last minus (total minus one)]. The insights you get from reading a book this way can be just as high impact as if you get the story as it unfolds.

For example, if you read this journal's first day, then its last day, then backwards through its substance, you would get a sense of my purpose, my lessons learned, and by reverse engineering, how I learned them. In the meantime, I'll have to let it unfold, though, through plain old straight-arrow psychological engineering, because I'm not even sure what lessons will be learned (if any). For me, it's like watching a movie (or better yet, a miniseries, stretched out across each day with no sense of direction but a looming, mirage-like sense of purpose that I'm sure is out there) dripping through my hand onto the paper. A movie dripping into being. I like that image.

Watching a movie as it drips into being.
11:48AM on 6/8/2010 from paper-journal

There are a myriad of gems in Pirsig's *Zen and the Art of Motorcycle Maintenance*. Like I said earlier (or maybe I just thought it – it's hard to tell when the little voice in your head *is* the voice) – this is one of those books I read almost 20 years ago. After re-reading, I can confirm what I remember from the first go-around: the book is about a guy taking a trip on a motorcycle with his kid, checking out scenery and other stuff, pontificating way too much about motorcycle parts, and then getting into some heady philosophy that's really too obtuse to be applicable to real life. Yeah, that's what I remember. But that was *16 year old me* doing the reading, and she was an entirely different person than 34 year old me who just finished reading this one again. My impression of the book is far more favorable now, but only because I have reached the bottom of my ocean. I've been on fast autopilot for many years, quickly moving from one experiment to another to "try it on" for size, only finding that not much really fits. And right now, I'm stuck in spiritual clothing that's too tight in the thighs, way too loose in the waist, and a little constrictive around the neck, with an itchy tag. (And by spiritual, I don't mean religious, where I typically wear one-size-fits-all free sizes very comfortably.)

And so finally, this little book is speaking to 34 year old me, and it's a book that is very conducive to reading in "reverse engineering" mode. And it attempts to resolve the divide between spirituality and technology – how apropos!

> "Reason was to be subordinate, logically, to Quality, and he was sure he would find the cause of its not being so back among the ancient Greeks, whose mythos had endowed our culture with the tendency underlying all

the evil of our technology, the tendency *to do what is 'reasonable' even when it isn't any good."*

Pirsig, *Zen and the Art of Motorcycle Maintenance*, p. 368

OK, so here's my review. Bla, bla, bla, heady Greek stuff, and then Pirsig comes out with the zinger: technology encourages us to do what is reasonable even when it's *not very good*. Meaning not soulful. I can't update my status every day in a completely *soulful* way. First of all, that would really expose my vulnerability, especially among certain members of my virtual world who, I've found (and despite their best and most honest intentions), tend to be covertly catty when you least expect it.

Add to that the self-censorship. I don't want to seem sad or depressed or needy or anything other than Super Fun Happy Me online, and quite frankly, that persona is only a glimmer of who I am. Twitter encourages us to tweet, and tells us it's the reasonable thing to do, because look what greatness others are getting out of the system! Same for Facebook. It has become *reasonable* in our day and age to independently, asynchronously, and one-size-fits-all communicate with those we love, those we like, and even those we just want (or happen to have) a superficial connection with. Everyone gets the same rations. Some people dig them. Most of them are just vapid and ashen; an illusion that just reminds you of food, rather than *being* it.

Realization: Soulful = Authentic

Years ago when I was living by myself one of my worst problems was getting the dishes done. So I came up with this idea of "dish entropy" – if you dirty one dish, then you must clean two. I'm going to apply the same technique to my Gmail Inbox except implemented with a little flair – every time I access Gmail, I'll force myself to delete or archive at least 10 old messages.

It may sound silly, but I need a new gimmick, and that's the role "dish entropy" will play. I've whittled the Inbox from 3,000 messages to only 1,100 in a little over a week, and the nervous energy that's been directed towards that activity is now waning. I haven't forgotten the first tenet of Inbox Zero...that is, to have zero distractions cluttering your Inbox.

> When I have no more distractions, wonder what it will be that will distract me?
> 3:54PM on 6/8/2010 from paper-journal

I have two emails from friends sitting in my Inbox right now, too, both a couple days fresh. Ironically, I'm frozen, and just can't answer them. Totally mute. I have things to say, and I definitely care about these people and value their friendship, but I'm temporarily paralyzed. Like a scorpion stung that spot in my brain that sends emails, and all I can do is sit on the floor, rigid, eyes wide open and going nowhere, until the venom recedes and I have words again, words that can be synchronously directed to others.

Cat's got your tongue. Scorpion's got your email. It's all the same, really.

> "There's nothing like a distant horizon to repair a shattered soul."
>
> Dane Gerhardt

> Alex has decided to sell water. He just hung up an "open" sign in the kitchen.
> 4:26PM on 6/8/2010 from paper-journal

So I got an email today with the subject line "How's Colorado?" – you know, the place where I'm fully relaxed and at peace, my place of power, the place where I decided to station myself in Google Latitude to become more centered. You know what?

Colorado (in my mind) is GREAT! Much better than where my body is right now, in central Virginia, but I'm going to let you think I'm physically in Colorado too, because if *two* people think it, then it's even *more* true. And I'm thankful you're helping me with my visualization. :)

Although I don't like to admit it, sometimes I feel like I'm falling apart. Disintegrating. Not *because* of the technology, but alongside it, splintering to so many places that I cease to exist as myself. But even puzzles have to be taken apart at times. They can't always sit on the table on display. At least the puzzle that's the inside of your head, and the inside of your being, can be assembled and reassembled as many times as you have the courage to tear it all down and start over. And when you do that, there's always a few extra pieces floating around that can change the whole picture, and make it shiny and new. Like Ram Dass said, technology just helps you unveil *the limits of the rational mind*, and sometimes it's by disintegrating your puzzle and forcing you to start over. Look at it with new eyes.

Of course, sometimes the puzzle itself is a wooden cube, oriented with one of its top corners pointing towards you, and laid out on a blue velvet cloth. You may spend years and years trying to solve it, even though there is only one piece; perhaps this is the very special way that you'll be able to confront the limits of your own rational mind.

2.2 mi and 20 odd geese to walkalajara and back.
8:36 PM on 6/8/2010 from paper-journal

6/9/2010 (Wednesday)

Slice, slice, slice. Got a couple more sections of my paper done after I woke up this morning. Having no expectations other than getting the next slice out of the way is definitely therapeutic. I'm not making the progress I'd _like_ to make, but I _am_ making progress.

It's time for preschool graduation!
9:38AM on 6/9/2010 from paper-journal

If my life had subtitles, you know, the ones that they flash on the bottom of the TV screen to let you know where or when a scene is taking place – the subtitle that would describe today is "The Joy of the Slice." Slice, slice, slice. That's all I've been doing today, and such a good day for it, because I haven't been able to mentally handle any more than a single slice at a time. I've spaced out twice today while driving… couldn't figure out where I was or where I was going… lost the security pass to get in the door at preschool… and in general, I'm having a hard time processing ordinary conversation. But in the oddest juxtaposition, I'm also now almost done with my ten-day-late paper. Slice, slice.

That's not all I sliced. I discovered today that you can slice _any_ activity to help get over mental blocks or motivation blocks (well maybe not _any_ activity, but my small sample is demonstrating some pretty effective results). For example, I sliced my messy car today. It's been cluttered since last fall… papers on the floor, crumpled up receipts, old eyeglass pieces, manila folders with stuff that was really critical to bring home and think about at one time (see how important those ended up being), statistics books (you know, just in case I ever need them on the road), CD cases, plastic hangers (just in case), a couple pillows, an old car seat (gee, I really should move that to the basement), a wool sweater, a few matchbox cars, two coats, a Rand McNally Road Atlas from 1996 that's missing most of the M and N States, one Daniel Pink book on motivation, a (tiny) bag of laundry I forgot to bring inside after my last business trip, and a whole bunch of lost things that have not yet been found.

I started slicing these one at a time, with no expectation of myself and no pressure on myself to slice any more than just one item at one moment. And before I knew it, I'd sliced about half the car, and now I'm almost free from the bondage that I created when I convinced myself I couldn't possibly start cleaning it 'til it got warm outside.

> Horseradish is good on everything.
> 7:15PM on 6/9/2010 from paper-journal

Oddly enough, as I spent my day slicing life to cope with the unfortunate explosion of my mental transformer earlier in the morning, and consequent inability to grasp more than a slice at a time, I felt *less lonely* than I've felt all these days since my disconnected experiment was launched. It was as if each little slice became my friend, holding my hand, letting me know that it would help boost my spirits, and so *immediately* too once the little slice was accomplished. My slice was my tiny little companion, then my next slice, then my next. When I wasn't slicing, I was sort of the antimatter of myself, blankly moving through space, staring through people and into the object behind them, admittedly a bit vacant. But that was only half the day.

> "It's paradoxical that where people are the most closely crowded... the loneliness is the greatest...

The explanation, I suppose, is that the physical distance between people has nothing to do with loneliness. It's psychic distances, and in Montana and Idaho the physical distances are big but the psychic distances between people are small, and here it's reversed...

There's this primary America of freeways and jet flights and TV and movie spectaculars. And people caught up in the primary America seem to go through huge portions of their lives without much consciousness of what's immediately around them. The media have convinced them that what's right around them is unimportant. And that's why they're lonely."

Pirsig, *Zen and the Art of Motorcycle Maintenance*, p. 366

The psychic distances between me and the little slices of life I embraced today, even the slice of taking three crumpled up receipts and tossing them into the trash at the gas station – they were very small. The Buddha was totally there in the trash can, and I mean that in the most honorable and respectful of ways. I found it, and it wasn't lonely when I was there with it and in it. And for a brief and fleeting and hours-long moment, I was free of all desires and there was no other place in the world I'd rather be than throwing away that little slice of trash.

I have had an immensely difficult time this week trying to keep up with what day it is. So far, I've had two Mondays, a Saturday, and a Thursday and a half. They keep changing on me, and not in the right order, either.

Conflating! *That's* the C word.

it used to be new mental models, now it's breaking out of my programmed identity.

63

9:31 PM on 6/9/2010 from paper-journal

They say that the words "nervous breakdown" have no meaning any more in the psychological and medical communities.
However, meaning is utterly personal, and it all depends upon
who you are.

6/10/2010 (Thursday)

Yahoo posted a story from space.com, published yesterday, entitled "More Active Sun Means Nasty Solar Storms Ahead". The sun has been quiet in recent times, report the scientists who study space weather, but we're about to hit a rough patch over the next few years.

> "Bad News for Gizmos: People of the 21st century rely on high-tech systems for the basics of daily life. But smart power grids, GIS navigation, air travel, financial services, and emergency radio communications can all be knocked out by intense solar activity."
> http://news.yahoo.com/s/space/20100609/sc_space/moreactionsunmeansnastysolarstormahead

Like the title says, that means bad news for our Droids and iPhones. Take note techies! I'm no doom and gloom soothsayer, but all of us might have to learn how to make do with our here-and-now lives, and rediscover our Self in its own immediate environment.

I've been deleting and archiving old Gmail with reckless abandon. Remember when I had 316 "new messages" in the Inbox? That's down to 18. Remember when I had over 3,000 regular messages in there? It's down to 548. Slice, slice. Whenever I look at my Gmail tab, I can't help but get the feeling that at it's all broken. I've been looking at a clogged box for nearly two years now. One sets one's own expectations, slowly, covertly, and without conscious awareness. When the Inbox is clean, I will undoubtedly feel naked.

> Finished my SPIE paper! Only 11 days late. 3.463 words, 10
> pgs. Woot.
> 9:51AM on 6/10/2010 from paper-journal

I feel relief. My paper is done. All of the anxiety and fearful-
ness and asking "will I ever *really* get it done?" are behind me.
It's hard to write a paper that you feel no sense of enthusiasm
about. Interestingly, the more slices I sliced, the more readily
I could get myself into another slice.

Realization: A feeling of success and accomplishment, no
matter how small, builds on itself and helps to make more
of the same feeling. (That's positive feedback, literally.)

I cannot claim for myself the genius that is the Slice Method.
This is completely attributable to Alistair Cockburn ("co-burn",
he clarifies on paper, regularly). He might have picked up method
from elsewhere, but he's the first person who introduced it to
me. Alistair is a software development process expert hailing
from Utah. He uses the slice method to help students (and even
software development professionals) learn the process of breaking down a software engineering problem into component parts.
In all of his years of working with software developers, he says
that (and I'm paraphrasing it here, so I hope I'm getting it right)
the biggest productivity block he's seen comes from this fundamental issue: breaking down a problem into slices. The Slice
Method helps people solve it.

Using the Slice Method, a programmer's first job is to outline
all of the steps of a problem in as tiny little pieces as possible –
thin, transparent slices – each of which demonstrates some sort
of progress or value or *immediate returns*. The idea is that you
bite off such a small part of the problem to be solved that you're
not overwhelmed by *taking* that step – it's *actionable*, meaning
you have the ability and mental clarity to get there – and as a
bonus, at the end of that step, you can prove to other people

(e.g. your manager) that you've been doing useful work and have not been wasting your time.

> @totheralistair slice, slice. Your method helped me break a major non-tech rut. Thx!
> 11:44AM on 6/10/2010 from paper-journal

I just achieved Inbox Zero. Then I checked http://quake.usgs.gov to see if that remarkable accomplishment triggered any earthquakes. None, not even in Asia.

My next step was to Google for "After Inbox Zero" because I am now void of my primary outlet for my nervous energy. Certainly, someone else will have reached the top of this mountain, and, being so adapted to the gradient path, would have wondered how to productively climb further. I would like to benefit from their knowledge. After searching for a while, I found an answer when I ran across http://www.productive flourishing. com/inbox-zero-is-overrated. Clearly, with a web site name like "productive flourishing," they've got to have it all figured out by now. Charlie is the productive, flourishing blogger.

> Just achieved Inbox Zero. Now what?
> 4:45PM on 6/10/2010 from paper-journal

According to Charlie, who blogged about this in October 2009, Inbox Zero is a waste of your time. He compares it to your laundry hamper. Who cares if you've got some clothes piling up? What are you, obsessive-compulsive, he asks? Dear Charlie: my laundry hamper does not have potentially available space of 7,464 MB like my Gmail. Laundry is a much smaller, and much more bounded, issue.

If clothing was data, how much laundry would 7,464 MB of it even represent? I vaguely remember pondering earlier whether I'd feel naked when there was nothing left in my Inbox. Maybe this is why.

(Answer: No, I don't actually feel naked. It just feels like my Inbox is *broken*, and so I'm slightly less inclined to want to *live* in it.)

Now that I've had a completely soul numbing productivity rut followed by tiny sparks of slice-driven accomplishment, my thoughts have turned to why I have been so intellectually under the weather. There are two possible paths to explore this: 1) The time honored tradition of "burn out," which is readily identified and well-researched, and 2) Pirsig's concept of "gumption killers." I'm still feeling a little too burned out myself to get too deeply into #1, so we'll put that on the shelf until later and maybe never. But #2... the gumption killers: Ego, Anxiety, Boredom, Impatience. Or E-BAI if it's a bit too hard to remember. (Sigh... off Twitter, off Facebook, and what do my thoughts do but turn to an auction site when I think of mnemonics. Sad.)

> "I like the word 'gumption' because it's so homely and forlorn and so out of style it looks as if it needs a friend and isn't likely to reject anyone who comes along... I like it also because it describes exactly what happens to someone who connects with Quality. He gets filled with gumption."
> Pirsig, *Zen and the Art of Motorcycle Maintenance*, p. 310

He goes on to explain that the Greek root for the word "enthusiasm" – *enthousiasmus* – translates as "filled with God." Gumption, then, is some sort of corn-fed inspiration, spiritually infused, that gives you the energy, the patience, and the wherewithal to meet your challenges head on... with calm resolve, to boot. What a great deal.

> "A person with gumption doesn't sit around dissipating and stewing about things. He's at the front of the train

of his own awareness, watching to see what's up the track and meeting it when it comes. That's gumption."
Pirsig, *Zen and the Art of Motorcycle Maintenance*, p. 310

I looooove that word *dissipating*. Dissipating, disintegrating, diluting, spreading out, covering more territory, become less and less concentrated until one moment you cease to be what you are and yield to the solvent in which you're swimming. Dissipating, wondering, drifting, separating, dancing from one hint of a focus to another – that's the natural state of the human mind, according to psychologist Mihaly Csikszentmihalyi: The natural state of human suffering is tied to this tendency. We'll spend more time with Mihaly's ideas later, but suffice it to say that if your mind is enjoying the natural human condition of wandering around aimlessly, you're going to have a hard time getting your "get up and go" to do its thing. (That's gumption too.)

> it's time for a Cerveza Pacifico
> 5:55PM on 6/10/2010 from paper-journal

Slice, slice! Just got my plane tickets to Denver and San Diego. I'm leaving in 12 days for a mini-tour around the country: 1 night in Greensboro, NC; 3 nights in Boulder, Colorado; 1 night in Los Angeles or the immediate vicinity; 5 nights in San Diego; 1 night returning home to Central Virginia. I'm starting to get excited about the trip. This is the first time I've felt excitement and anticipation since graduation weekend one month ago, when I jubilantly celebrated my one-year anniversary of joining the professorhood.

Excitement. Anticipation. The contentment of knowing I've just committed to a trip where solitude and new horizons and old horizons are all part of the gift. Slice, slice.

6/11/2010 (Friday)

It's been 12 full days since I checked Twitter or Facebook. The suspense, the unknowing about what my contacts are working on and enjoying, is like an orange muddy water flowing slowly under me. It used to be flowing much, much faster... but it was less muddy then too, and there's no way to ascertain which would be better or worse. The only remedy is to slice a little more of where-I-am life.

> Cop pulls over physicist: "know how fast you were going?"
> Ans: "no, but I know where I am"
> 10:17AM on 6/11/2010 from paper-journal

So back to the subject of productivity killers... gumption traps... things that get in the way of enjoying the here and now and making progress while doing it. The first one, according to Pirsig, is "Ego". The idea here is that if you think too highly of your own capabilities and expertise, you're going to overlook potentially critical details that will prevent you from being able to solve problems. Mihaly's take on ego (and I'll call him Mihaly for convenience since Csikszentmihalyi tends to get stuck in the throat) is a little different, and derives from the views of the psychologist William James:

> "The problem is that the more the ego becomes identified with symbols outside the self the more vulnerable it becomes... To prevent its annihilation, the ego forces us to be constantly on the watch for anything that might threaten the symbol on which it relies. Our view of the world becomes polarized into 'good' and 'bad'; to the

71

first belong those things that support the image of the self, to the second, those that threaten it. This is how the third veil of Maya works: it distorts reality so as to make it congruent with the needs of the ego."

Csikszentmihalyi, *The Evolving Self*, p. 79

Blend Pirsig and Mihaly, though, and a really distinct message emerges: if ego is all in the business of self-proliferation, and aggressively defending the *symbols* upon which it relies, then ironically, *the ego keeps us disconnected from our true self.* And it's all so nefarious, because thanks to the ego's virus-like skills of self preservation, we never even notice that this stuff is going on. We think the symbols *are* our true selves, when the self is actually hanging out by the side of some *other* country road still waiting for a ride.

This explains why the ego is a gumption (or productivity) trap: if it keeps us from truly identifying with what's deepest inside us, our Self (completely unadulterated by the symbols that propel the ego) – then ego is also orange cones and striped horses, a shimmering roadblock that interferes with the path to *enthousiasmos*. If we really want to tap into that perpetual motion machine of inspiration, that source of free-flowing energy, that push that will get us out the door and into the car and joyously running our errands – we've got to take out our shovels, start digging, and recover that true self from underneath all the dusty and gravelly layers of ego.

It's much easier said than done, and I can't admit that I'd even know where to *find* the shovel to commence this sort of digging. But it provides an interesting clue: if you're having trouble getting something going, starting a new task or just trying to pick yourself up and start something over again – *what's your motivation?* Are you feeding and propagating the symbols that your ego is currently defined by, or are you really being spurned on by some genuine pocket of authenticity in your soul? If you answered the latter, you'll have a much easier time tapping into the natural energy source that will make you productive.

skin-tingly word of the day: antipodean. concerning points opposite one another on the earth.
11:13AM on 6/11/2010 from paper-journal

A tiny postscript to that last discussion: you might say, hold it! I get a lot of energy for my ego-driven activities – my ego is pretty darn motivated! And indeed it is. The only problem is that the ego-driven energy really isn't sustainable. It will burn you out, or burn other people up, or maybe even both, all while keeping your Self conveniently buried alive.

i'm in a fmd. fully meaningful deliberation.
3:48PM on 6/11/2010 from paper-journal

The next challenge on the list of productivity traps – drive traps – is *Anxiety*, according to Pirsig. He says it's the opposite of overconfident ego:

> "You're so sure you'll do everything wrong you're afraid to do anything at all. Often this rather than 'laziness' is the real reason you find it hard to get started. The gumption trap of anxiety, which results from overmotivation, can lead to all kinds of errors of excessive fussiness."
> Pirsig, *Zen and the Art of Motorcycle Maintenance*, p. 322

I am particularly guilty of anxiety, and in fact, I've often assumed it's just one of those personality traits that makes me who I am. And, I'm not selective with my anxiety either – I've got plenty of it for any situation that needs it, and for many situations that *don't*, as well. I also have an immense amount of laziness, which I've always framed positively to convince myself that's why I'm so inspired by the field of quality management (what I got my

Ph.D in). After all, if you build something right the first time with quality, you avoid a lot of future problems, and lazy people would rather not deal with problems in the present *or* in the future, especially those that are unnecessary and can be prevented. The field of quality management is also concerned with *continuous improvement* and the relentless pursuit of performance excellence. Better, faster, more cost effective, more efficient, more lean, higher impact! These are siren songs for the lazy yet inspired manager (a role I played for several years).

So Pirsig says it's not the laziness that interrupts your flow and impales your get up and go – it's anxiety. You're too concerned with the details. Too fuzzy. Too exacting. You're working yourself up about all those details, and they're stifling you before you have a chance to begin work.

Those who know me well (and even those who I just have a cursory relationship with) will immediately notice an elephant-size discrepancy in the description of the anxiety-ridden details freak. *This is not me.*

I, in contrast, am an anxiety-ridden strategist. *You* can worry about the details if you like – whether we have enough gas, or oil, or what speed we're going, or where to turn next – I'll worry about whether we're headed to the right *country*, and whether we should be flying rather than driving. If anxiety is my gumption trap, it's unrelated to my connection with the details, because I certainly don't worry about them. I delegate that worry. Give me the forest. You can have all the trees.

Consequently, I pondered where that anxiety could be coming from for a person like me, and found a consistent source: *overwhelmingness.* When you are a strategy person, you may not become anxious over the details of a problem, but you'll certainly become unraveled as you shove the entire complexity of the issue into a single moment of time, and try to deal with it there.

Dealing with complex problems is one of those activities that is tremendously benefitted by the passage of time. The more time you have, the more space and freedom is available to let the solutions unfold organically, and *without causing stress or anxiety*. A healthy respect for (and appreciation of) time and how you can use it to your advantage can help defeat overwhelmingness for strategists, and detail-anxiety for tacticians. If you are in both camps, then you should just pick the remedy that feels the most useful for the situation at hand.

> it's time for another cerveza pacifico
> 5:14PM on 6/11/2010 from paper-journal

Ron (@rduplain) and I talked a bit today about how my disconnected experiment is going, and ego, and self, and progress. I told him about Inbox Zero, and Charlie the blogger's laundry comment. "Those naysayers don't get it," he said. "It's not about having nothing in your Inbox...it's about having as little as possible hanging over your head so you can *get out there and live!*" Right on, dude.

> New 5.0 earthquake 960 mi NE of Auckland
> 5:51PM on 6/11/2010 from paper-journal

Boredom and impatience will have to wait for another day.

6/12/2010 (Saturday)

Yesterday, Ron handed me the *Lifehacker* book by Gina Trapani and told me it was time to revisit Chapters 2 and 6. He said I'd be ready for their wisdom. I've read the book before, and it was very cool with amazing tips and tricks about how to streamline your work on the computer and online, but I can't say it ever set me on fire before.

This time, it didn't take me 10 seconds into Chapter 2 to become inspired, to relate to the story, to extract a gem of recognition from the prose. I am not alone! There are others like me!

> "Your attention is your most endangered resource... limitless amounts of information always available at the press of a button... vie for your attention. But there are a finite number of minutes, hours, and days in your life...
>
> Further, email software and cell phones and instant messenger make you reachable and interruptible at any moment in time... this type of interruption-driven existence can have a devastating effect on your mental focus and your ability to perform. It makes for workers who are irritated, overwhelmed, and run ragged."
>
> Trapani, *Lifehacker*, p. 29

An interrupt-driven existence. That's it! Somewhere, somehow over these past several years of pervasive technology and ubiquitous connectedness, I've become convinced (and I'm sure I'm not the only one here) that quickly responding to incoming requests is a public demonstration of my efficiency, rapid turn-around, and commitment and dedication to the task. I'm *on it*, people. Can't you see what a high performing worker I am?

I can imagine Pirsig and Mihaly sitting here in my dining room with me as I recite the last paragraph. They exchange smirks, knowing glances... one of them even tries to choke back a grin. All Pirsig can see is how distant I am from my true motivations, how I'd rather be somewhere else, anywhere but here. Mihaly senses the shroud of ego, the third veil of Maya, the maker of that distance Pirsig initially recognized. As a psychologist, Mihaly has held sessions with many people who have rediscovered, and uncovered, the relationships between their unconscious actions and their ego – and yet it's a fresh new discovery each time. He never tires of it.

> I was up at 4:30am and conquered the urge to tweet –
> even on paper!
> 9:09AM on 6/11/2010 from paper-journal

There's even a name for the condition brought about by living an interrupt-driven existence: ADT. Even though it sounds like a powerful pesticide that you wouldn't want to get in your socks, it actually stands for "Attention Deficit Trait." Trapani quotes an article by psychologist Edward Hallowell, who named the condition:

> "It's a condition induced by modern life, in which you've
> become so busy attending to so many inputs and out-
> puts that you become increasingly distracted, irritable,
> impulsive, restless, and over the long-term, underachiev-
> ing. In other words, it costs you efficiency because
> you're doing so much or trying to do so much, it's as if
> you're juggling one more ball than you possibly can."
> Alorie Gilbert, "Why Can't You Pay Attention
> Anymore?" CNet News, 10/22/2008, as cited by
> Trapani, *Lifehacker,* p. 30

The one symptom of ADT that they forgot to mention, and this is the one that comes after the distraction, irritability, impulsiveness and restlessness – is numbness. Sometimes the numb part can coexist with the other symptoms. It's especially dangerous when numbness and impulsiveness get together because that's when you make really intelligent decisions (read: *not*) and sometimes even your ego can get kind of affronted. When your ego raises its eyebrows at you, that's a sign something is wrong (and not typically indicative of progress).

It makes me feel better that there's a name for this condition, because that means it can be ritually exorcised. Without a name, you can call it and call it in an effort to address it directly, but you'll get no answer.

> Starting my new medicine today...the stuff that will help me get my reflexes back
> 9:39AM on 6/12/2010 from paper-journal

So how do you fix ADT? What is the appropriate ritual? Trapani, thankfully, has an answer to that too. She points at Mihaly, who's still conferring with Pirsig silently at my dinner table, displaying a contented and wise countenance and waiting for us to uncover the next truth.

> "The key to overcoming ADT is to fully focus on one task at a time. Give yourself the time and space to dig into a problem and reach that state of mind called *flow*, when you're fully immersed in your task, effortlessly successful, and oblivious to time and other external factors."
> Trapani, *Lifehacker*, p. 30

Flow. The mere mention of the word makes my skin tingle, as if dancing through shallow, fragrant waterfalls in Hawaii, swimming with lumbering turtles in long slow sinusoids in the vertical, the bliss radiating isotropically from being as my spirit harmonizes with the world around me. It's like a drug, one that combines the relaxation and primordial soup of opium with the power and strength of steroids. Mihaly spent his whole professional career studying this state of *optimal experience*.

But I'm getting ahead of myself. We can't get into flow until we get rid of all the cobwebs and veils. And we still have to discuss the productivity traps of Boredom and Impatience. (I'm specifically holding off, to defend, rather recursively, against the latter. The more pressure on me, the slower I'll go!)

In the meantime, I really should send Breanna a Facebook message and see if she wants to go to the pool. (Sigh... can't do that. What's her phone number?)

6/13/2010 (Sunday)

Today has included a watershed moment. I have now spent almost 24 hours offline – disconnected from my connected media *as well as* this journal, which has been serving as a proxy for my nervous online habit. I did not accomplish such a feat on my own: Todd and I had friends over for the afternoon and for dinner, and I discovered just how whole the distraction of good company can be.

> Excellent time w @stuartdleitch and @kristylmoon grilling veggies and sampling wines!
> 8:49AM on 6/13/2010 from paper-journal

A few weeks ago, I would have been simultaneously steeped in the online and virtual worlds. We'd be sitting outside on the deck in cheerful conversation, and I'd check Twitter every 15 minutes or so, and maybe even update everyone on some interesting trivia that a mutual friend had tweeted. This time? I was only having conversation with the people around me, and it was totally sufficient, and thicker in density too. I have received the first glimmer of the answer to my fundamental question: "If I disconnect from my virtual life, will I reconnect with my REAL one?"

> Headed to the Russells' moving-to-Germany party
> 2:14AM on 6/13/2010 from paper-journal

I feel paralyzed today. It seems my only slices have been to wake up, shower, make coffee and try to figure out what today's slices *should* be. Only three of four can be considered successful. Perhaps I am struggling with one of the two remaining productivity traps.

Boredom. Am I bored right now? Yes, definitely. I have plenty to do, but I don't want to do any of it, and so I am punctuated. My lack of *want* stems from two things: 1) my energy has been drained by keep-the-family-running tasks this morning, small ones, like the mental battle of trying to get the 5-year old to eat something that's remotely nutritious, and 2) it just seems like that first step of anything, that first slice, requires more energy than I can afford given the initial constraint. Nothing on my invisible list is actionable, that is, I don't have the mental and emotional and physical resources to get going on that first slice. Not actionable. I can't just get started immediately because the first slice of any of my task is obscured by something, something that is as of yet unidentified.

Pirsig's boredom is a little different. He says boredom means something *else* that your soul needs to be working on with a higher priority is just looming overhead, and that you just haven't recognized it yet. Boredom is a symptom that "your gumption supply is low and must be replenished before anything else is done." He recommends that you indulge in the ritual and repetitive aspects of the boring task, appreciating their familiarity. But this assumes that you can actually get started.

My boredom right now is different than Pirsig's, but may have the same root cause: low reserves. When your emotional gas tank is sputtering, it's a realistic concern to think you might not have the energy to get going on a task, and in the consequent self-perpetuating state, there's nothing left to do but sit in the void. And it is *void*. Lacking form or structure, or even a well-defined parking lot.

> last night's spider bite on my thigh is turning purple. is this bad?
> 2:40PM on 6/13/2010 from paper-journal

His preliminary remedy for boredom is simple: sleep. Although I do recall being bored when I woke up this morning, so it's possible there may be a slight gap in that theory. One thing is for sure though… boredom is definitely a productivity trap. It has claimed 6 to 8 of my hours today, and imbued me with a seemingly indomitable sadness since I can't even pull together the energy to start an argument with it.

Sleep, ritual, actionability. These are three potential remedies for breaking the rut of boredom. I might try out a little of the first one… anything would be better than the way I spent a couple of my bored hours this morning: sitting behind my computer screen trying to actively resist the temptation to check Facebook. This is ordinarily something I've done to distract myself from boredom, rather than seeking out and repairing the root cases of the boredom. That's real smart – sitting in from of your computer, disengaged, trying not to use it.

(Despite the vacuous silliness of the scenario, I'm happy to report that in the battle between me and boredom, I emerged victorious, having simply walked away from my screen.)

Sleep. Vitamins. Aspirin. Hope.

> What doesn't kill you usually works on the 2nd attempt –
> Mr. Krabs
> 4:40PM on 6/13/2010 from paper-journal

The fourth and final trap is Impatience. This trap is similar to boredom, and according to Pirsig, it results from not allocating enough time for a task. If you feel that your time is insufficient or cut short, your natural reaction is impatience:

> "Impatience is best handled by allowing an indefinite time for the job, particularly new jobs that require unfamiliar techniques by doubling the allotted time when

> circumstances force time planning; and by scaling down
> the scope of what you want to do."
> Pirsig, *Zen and the Art of Motorcycle Maintenance*, p. 325

Impatience confounds productivity because it *dilutes focus*.
Instead of being in the here and now solving this moment's slice
of the puzzle, you are *in all moments*, and as a result, can't complete *any* slices. You are rejecting the luxury given to you by the
passage of time: to become introduced to the various facets of
a problem or task or issue in a gentle, non-threatening way, an
unfolding that invites you to connect with the scenario and the
opportunity to become immersed in it.

In summary, there are four productivity traps and a host of
potential remedies:

Trap	Remedies
Ego	Modesty, skepticism, openness to possibilities
Anxiety	Rescind overmotivation, adapt or reset expectations
Boredom	Sleep, ritual, actionability, coffee
Impatience	Set no deadline or *time-based* expectations

I'm not too haunted by ego as a productivity killer, although
sometimes it can be a continuous improvement killer – it's a
little disappointing when I work really hard at something and yet
there's still an ocean of improvement opportunities right out the
gate (that other people tune into immediately). I can easily get
over that, though.

Anxiety is probably the bane of my unproductive existence. I
condense each frontier into a single point in time, of neutron
star density, resisting the opportunities that *time itself* builds into
the human process of problem solving. Because time unfolds,

we don't have to solve things all at once – we don't have to know how the story is going to end. Anxiety feeds into impatience, bilaterally, although usually this is a function of a network of relationships. Managers trapped by Impatience and maybe Ego tend to breed workers plagued by Anxiety and Boredom. It's all interconnected.

Boredom is a killer for me personally, and it's an offshoot and direct result of anxiety. If I can't get over the hump and get something started, why bother? And then there's nothing to do, and boredom sets in, and then some more impatience – because think of all the things you could get done, if only you weren't wallowing in your own boredom!

Flow solves this problem. Flow solves all problems. Getting into flow, however, *is* the problem – but fortunately, also, the *sparkling solution*.

spider bite purple is fading to magenta. i think i'll survive
9:04PM on 6/13/2010 from paper-journal

85

6/14/2010 (Monday)

It's Day 15 (or 14 if you consider that we started this experiment on June 1st). I think we started on May 31st, so today will be Day 15. That means two more days until the tension bursts into Something Entirely Unexpected.

> i love finding something you thought was so lost you stopped looking for it.
> 11:26AM on 6/14/2010 from paper-journal

I've been thinking a lot over the past few days about the relationship between pain and expectations. I started on my new dose of medicine – the doctor's giggly response to my lack of reflexes in the knees and elbows – just a few days ago. What I learned is that the lack of deep tendon reflexes (and I'm not a doctor, so I might completely foul up the medical accuracy of this) is a sign, or can be a sign, that your neurons aren't firing properly. When you identify the underlying condition, provide the body with the chemicals its missing, then those neural connections will form again. For some people, this can be as simple as restoring the balance through vitamins, or healthy eating, or exercise. For me, it meant bumping up my medication for an autoimmune disorder I've had most of my life.

Here's my **Realization**: Sometimes you don't even know you've been experiencing pain until that pain is removed, and you feel what it's like to be without pain – then you can create a contrast in your mind and appreciate the experience of being pain-free.

Chronic pain over a long enough period of time dulls the senses, inflames the nerves. For months, I've had intense pain in my right foot and left arm and hand. In my foot, it was like a deep, rigid burning, a stiffness that crawled up the ankle at night to indulge in flesh-eating all the way up to the knee. My left hand has been in a bipolar state between numbness on the skin, sometimes in the knuckles and other times in the forearm or elbow, and the subterranean ache of an impending radius and ulna earthquake. It's been difficult to grip things, challenging to keep my balance on my feet, and in retrospect, painful. But I only recognized the pain the morning I woke up without it. I had convinced myself that it wasn't really that bad, I can deal with it, and it's probably just from taking too many long walks or writing or typing too much. Meanwhile, the pain is hanging out getting more and more frustrated with my lack of awareness: "Hey! We've got a problem here! Your neurons are melting down, and I'm trying to help you out and let you know, and you're just ignoring me! What's your problem?"

The problem was that my expectations had gradually shifted to the point where my pain was a normal part of my daily existence. Because I expected to feel the pain, I became consciously unaware of its presence, its constrictive and instructive relationship with me, and what it was trying to say.

There's a whole branch of medical study dedicated to pain, and the phenomena that surround the experience of pain. It's called algology in older medical dictionaries. The word derives from the Greek word algo, meaning pain (not to be confused with the Latin alg-, meaning seaweed). Of course, I guess if you got caught in a twisted mass of seaweed, that might be painful, too, if there was enough seaweed. In addition to constricting you, it might even be suffocating.

Algol is also an eclipsing binary star in Perseus. Its Arabic name, al-Ghul, means "the demons," and its mythology is tied in with

Medusa losing her head to the sword of Perseus. The symbol is also related to the anglicized word "alcohol" which can serve at times to extract a person from the reasonable senses he or she possesses. Algol... algology... pain... losing one's head. When we are in pain, we can lose our heads and our senses of reason; we can behave unpredictably and erratically until the source of the pain is removed, or until the narcotics kick in. Alternatively, we can lose our heads in the subtlest of ways, denying the pain's message until the symptoms are oppressed or buried, while the damage is being done. But if we were really smart, we would work *with* the pain to uncover hidden gems that tell us how to live better, and more free, and more authentically. Rather than losing our heads, pain can help us get back in our heads and grow our selves, if we can distinguish the sensation of the pain from the subjective experience of it.

> "From a phenomenological perspective, the distinction between pain behavior, the experience of pain, and the emotional states accompanying pain, such as suffering or demoralization, is highly ambiguous."
>
> *Good, Pain as Human Experience*, p. 139

No wonder pain can make you lose your head, all shackled together inextricably with your emotions like that. In any case, the point of this story is that these unclear boundaries motivated Good to do a research study on "cognitive restructuring" – that is, helping patients change the way they think about pain – to see if their perception of pain would be improved and whether they would experience a reduction in symptoms. It worked. Expectation influenced both the perception and experience of pain.

I think it would be trite and inappropriate to suggest that disconnecting from technology has caused or is causing me pain. There's definitely some sort of emotional pull when I think about just checking my Google Chat for one second, or just see-ing what people are doing on Facebook today (just *today*). But it's not physical pain, just emotional discomfort.

On the other hand, as I look back over the past few months, it's pretty clear that technology and my virtual self had pulled me out of my body to the extent where I wasn't feeling the physical pain I needed to – so it could be identified and get repaired. Is this direct experiential evidence of the narcotic nature of social media? Ten days ago, when I wrote that "what I recognize is that the nervous habit has been obscuring other problems that I need to uncover and deal with," never did I anticipate that there was a stark physical issue lurking just beneath the surface.

> to the hypnotist, the pharmacy, and to pick up a new bottle of lavender soap... yum
> 12:56PM on 6/14/2010 from paper-journal

I had forgotten to mention earlier why detecting the physical pain of neural issues is so important: if the neurons aren't firing right in your arms and legs, what makes you think they're fir-ing properly in your brain? Exactly. The body and the mind are linked physically, and if there's a physical issue, the mind is bound to be suffering as well. *Mens sana in corpore sano.* Sound mind in a sound body. I'll have to remind myself of this next time I'm doing sit-ups.

Some of you are probably wondering by now why in the world I'm spending time with a hypnotist this summer. Maybe I'll tell that whole story later. Suffice it to say, right now, that it's a really interesting way to learn conscious relaxation, where you actually get to think thought while you're deeply relaxed. There's really nothing magical or mystical about it, except the part where you can recall amazing tiny details of past experiences, details that you don't have access to when you're just "remembering." Oh, and the other curious aspect of hypnosis is that you're basically *suggested into a flow state*. But again, I'm getting ahead of myself. It's not time to flow until all the cobwebs are gone, the veils are lifted, and we have a mechanism in place for staying cobweb-free.

got my first section done for the 2010 Baldrige independent review tonight... whew!
9:56PM on 6/14/2010 from paper-journal

I was very productive tonight, and although I now have a headache from it all, here's the recipe that made me successful: 1) Avoid the Impatience Trap by reducing my own expectations: I know this piece is due tonight, but I'm going to give myself unlimited time to finish it, and if it doesn't get done, I'll tap into my "unlimited time" equity. 2) Avoid the Boredom trap by treating this review process as a comfortable ritual. 3) Take aspirin for headache pain.

Good night.

6/15/2010 (Tuesday)

Until yesterday afternoon, Daniel Pink's book *Drive* had lain dormant on the back seat of my Tahoe, where it's been driven itself for at least a couple thousand miles as I accumulated the motivation to begin reading it. Those clues inside, the ones that reveal how to get more in touch with your own intrinsic motivation (I hope), were of no use to me as the book passively lay next to the carseat, covers unturned. Now, awakened from what could have become a sticky plastic summer tomb (Alex has a tendency to drip his Capri Sun in rather Pollock-esque patterns), the book has life and I'll start reading it today. I can't believe that I didn't have the motivation to start reading the motivation book. (Boredom block, definitely... with a little bit of recursion for flavor.)

> My spider bite is now the size of a sand dollar... how can you tell if these things are poisonous?
> 8:52AM on 6/15/2010 from paper-journal

I had a very structured day yesterday. Had a few appointments here and there mid-day, some things I had to pick up along the way, and all on a relatively constrained schedule. It was far easier to get beyond the productivity traps with this little bit of structure in place for me – it wasn't an oppressive structure that caused anxiety to set in, but a very instructive guideline for how to get involved in the activities of the day, and how to increase the potential for entering into a flow state.

As if you can't tell, *flow* is the drug that I'm ultimately after. Maybe I'm not an adrenaline junkie: maybe I'm just a *flow* junkie.

As I evolve through this process of discovery, I am now aware that I'll have to find a way to prevent flow from becoming my next idol, my next chain link in the unending circle of chasing new desires. That will be an interesting balance to identify and maintain!

Structure is essential. Pirsig alerts us that flow is insistent on that structure:

> "You can't live on just groovy emotions alone. You have to work with the underlying form of the universe too, the laws of nature which, when understood, can make work easier, sickness rarer, and famine almost absent."
> Pirsig, *Zen and the Art of Motorcycle Maintenance*, p. 300

I spent five years of my life studying quality and innovation in the context of managing technology. One thing that really stood out to me in the process of learning about these topics was *why* quality systems are important. Now, the whole concept of quality systems itself can be kind of confusing – there are strategic systems like the Baldrige criteria, and operational systems like ISO 9000, and industry-specific systems (or at least ones that started out that way) like the CMMI. There are acronyms *everywhere*, and whenever so many acronyms gather together in one place, you can be certain that they've formed a secret society and you'll need to endure a tense period of hazing before it is revealed to you that the secrets are obvious.

A quality system is just a collection of processes – things that you do. When you know what the steps of these processes are, when you know how they relate to one another, and you also know how to systematically and repeatably *do* them (even if you're plagued by a memory lapse, or if someone has to step in and do your job for you), you've started. Then, when you know how to check and see whether all those processes together are meeting some overall goals, and you've made a commitment to continuously review and improve them, you have all the essential elements of a quality system. (That is, a quality system as they are viewed today, in 2010.)

I have a little issue with this purely mechanistic approach, which is summed up as follows: 1) Quality systems provide structures; a way to work with underlying forms. 2) Flow provides access to those groovy emotions that Pirsig mentioned. There is no requirement (or thought) at the moment for a quality system to help those involved in carrying out their processes tap into all the groovy emotions, and use them to achieve the goals of the quality system more authentically and effortlessly.

What? You say you don't work with any quality systems… that you're not an employee of a manufacturing plant or something? Well how about this: do you have a morning routine? For example: 1) Wake up at 6:30am. 2) Go downstairs, pop 6 scoops of coffee into the machine, put in water, press "ON." 3) Check email. 4) Take shower. 5) Spot check… is it 7am yet? Am I still on time? 6) Get dressed. 7) Go downstairs, drink coffee. 8) Feed kids breakfast. 9) Get kids clothed and shoed. 10) Pack lunch. 11) Get to work by 8:30am. This is not my morning routine, but it could be someone's. In any case, it's a quality system, because it has systematic and repeatable steps, it helps you to not forget anything, and it helps you to get to work and school on time (a quality attribute, and indeed, one of the critical success factors for this process). Much of this process can even be considered a ritual, especially if you eat the same thing for breakfast each morning.

Realization: Form underlies flow.

There's still a bit of a problem here with my experiment, with Project Disconnected. And that is: that this was never intended to be a permanent denial of technology. I like Twitter, I like Facebook, and oh my, I so miss online chat right now. There are nice things that can enhance my life if I weave them into the *structure* of my personal quality system, rather than letting them weave me. If I want to achieve the nirvana of flow, at least a little bit every day, I'm going to have to rescind this interrupt-driven existence while I continue to embrace my technology, at least platonically — because by definition, *flow is not interrupted.*

"The way to solve the conflict between human values and technological needs is not to run away from technology. That's impossible. The way to resolve the conflict is to break down the barriers of dualistic thought that prevent a real understanding of what technology is — not an exploitation of nature, but a fusion of nature and the human spirit into a new kind of creation that transcends both... this transcendence should also occur at the individual level, on a personal basis, in one's own life, in a less dramatic way."

Pirsig, *Zen and the Art of Motorcycle Maintenance*, p. 298

Kitten w/2 faces born in Charleston, WV: http://www.wvga-zette.com/News/201006110918
12:52PM on 6/15/2010 from paper-journal

Walked 2.04mi to Foods of All Nations & back... now, Gerolsteiner time
2:02PM on 6/15/2010 from paper-journal

"A fusion of nature and the human spirit into a new kind of creation that transcends both..." — wow, that's beautiful. It makes so much sense. Just develop some sort of healthy symbiotic fusion between your soul and your technology, and your technology can uplift your soul and help you connect with Self, and all of a sudden, transcendence occurs. Beautiful, but completely *not actionable*! I don't know how to get started, I wouldn't know how to keep this transcendence transcending (which is a sustainability question), and I wouldn't know how to tell whether transcendence was happening in the first place (that's a question of evaluation and assessment).

Has anybody seen that guy in #cville with the giant stuffed tarantula on the back of his VW bug?
5:55PM on 6/15/2010 from paper-journal

Here's an interesting revelation that has nothing to do with anything: did you know that the Latin words *alma mater*, which you usually think of as meaning "the college that you graduated from," actually means "nourishing mother"? And that the term *alma mater*, in ancient Rome, was used to refer to any one of the mother goddesses? That's pretty cool. It's like saying "Penn State is my mother goddess."

As I'm sitting here at the table in my dining room, thinking about that potential fusion between technology and soul, I'm feeling a steady *pull* towards Facebook. *That will give me something to do,* I'm thinking, the seductive whisper of the temptation sitting on my shoulder. The angel on my other shoulder cringes. "She hasn't kicked the habit yet... leave her alone!" Checking the latest earthquake status, albeit slightly obsessive, has just not been satisfying my social need. (A ha! Social *need*... that's the problem!) I think in Part II of my experiment I may need to choose some new structures that eliminate my perception that social needs are definitively satisfied online. Oh, and the earthquakes are going to have to go, too.

> "The mechanism of most addictive drugs is to send a fusillade of dopamine to the nucleus accumbens. The feeling delights, then dissipates, then demands another dose. In other words, if we watch how people's brains respond, promising them monetary rewards and giving them cocaine, nicotine, or amphetamines looks disturbingly similar. This could be one reason that paying people to stop smoking often works in the short run. It replaces one (dangerous) addiction with another (more benign) one."
>
> Pink, *Drive*, p. 55

Like I was saying, the earthquakes are just going to have to go. That will be part of my updated Rules of Engagement for Part II. What's also going to have to go is this vacant "sitting in front of the computer waiting for something to happen" state of being. It reminds me of people who open their refrigerators every ten minutes waiting for something new to mysteriously manifest. Unless you live in the Matrix, that's a long shot (and even there, they might not even *have* refrigerators).

Realization: Replacing one addiction with another is a very subtle, nefarious, and almost involuntary process.

> Son of a meteorologist :) "look mommy, I got a moderate rain colored (orange) popsicle" -Alex
> 7:43PM on 6/15/2010 from paper-journal

> Can I subcontract anyone to deal with this raging 5yr old's fit? Zero rationality.
> 10:33PM on 6/15/2010 from paper-journal

6/16/2010 (Wednesday)

We're out of coffee, and I'm angry. Why does it seem like I'm the only person in this household who cares about (err, I mean *notices*) when we run out of *important staples*? Now we're out of bottled water and coffee, which just tacks one more thing onto my to-do list. Grrrrr. Ordinarily, I wouldn't mind about the water, but I'm allergic to the stuff that comes out of the tap in my house. A few days of drinking it, and I break out with hives on my face and chest. It's a consequence that's entirely preventable.

There is indeed a silver lining though, and it is called *Wu-Yi Oolong tea*. It's dark, smoky, and just a little more emotionally dangerous than coffee. And the silky plastic mesh tea bags that it comes in are perfectly elegant, down to their three dimensional triangularness and the way they can so heroically stand up to themselves.

> Wu-yi Oolong tea on a cool central VA morning
> 8:59AM on 6/16/2010 from paper-journal

Most of my journey so far has centered around getting rid of the stumbling blocks that prevent a person from achieving flow (which we still haven't defined, but I bet you instinctively already know what it is). And those blocks can be pretty well summed up by Pirsig's gumption killers and Mihaly's veils. I've talked about the productivity killers (Ego, Boredom, Anxiety, and Impatience) pretty extensively, but I've neglected the whole veils concept, and if we're going to reach the nirvana of flow, these too must be removed. Like Pirsig's conceptualization, the veils are killers too, but of a different nature: they kill one's ability to *see out of the box.* Thus, the shroud of a veil can prevent a person from getting to the root cause of, and resolving, a productivity killer.

Mihaly focuses on the three "veils of Maya" in his work. In Sanskrit, *maya* means "illusion," or more literally, "not what it is." When you confront an illusion, it's not really what you think it is. So when you're faced with a challenge, the lesson of the veils is that you have to examine what's really going on underneath the surface. You have to solve the root cause of the problem rather than some illusory "red herring" style symptom. The veils get in the way of seeing the problem clearly, and simultaneously paralyze your ability to respond in accurate and effective ways.

The three veils of Maya, according to Mihaly, are genes, culture and ego. The way to see if you're being influenced by one of these three veils is to ask yourself this very simple question: "What's your motivation?"

> At #cville @getopenspace for the first time in over a month
> 10:54AM on 6/16/2010 from paper-journal

Sometimes, you're driven by forces and mental models that are not only outside of your Self, but may also be completely anathema to who you really are. Figuring this out – in fact, becoming aware of the subconscious structures and illusions that make you do things, think about things a certain way, react to situations, and even *avoid* situations – is no trivial task. It's kind of like asking you to become aware that your perception of the world is inextricably linked to the cultural assumptions made during the thousands of years that your primary language developed. That's just too big to load into a lone person's brain, let alone their understanding.

> "Even if a man has learned not to act out... impulses, much of his inner life, much of his psychic energy, is

tied down in emotions and thoughts prompted by instinct."

Csikszentmihalyi, *The Evolving Self*, p. 64

Instinct. It's a natural tendency, a pattern of programming so tightly bound up in your body, that it's no wonder you might confuse certain instinctual leanings for the constitution of your *self*. Eating, sleeping, satisfying biological urges or compulsions, making yourself more attractive (and possibly less stinky) to wield a little more power and dominance over the other people in your environment... it's all programmed by your genes to facilitate survival and reproduction.

There is most certainly the influence of the genetic veil not only over the *people* who use Twitter, but also the *tweets* that they think they alone produce and control. Just as the prehistoric human existed continuously on the lookout for threats, to engage in either fight or flight for the promotion of survival, Twitter facilitates the same behavior. With Twitter, you can sit up on your hill, continuously scanning the digital landscape for predators, people encroaching on your territory (both professional and romantic), or large groups of organized invaders (that's called "competitive intelligence"). From your elevated vantage point, you might even be able to identify new opportunities for gaining resources through either wit or plundering. Add to this that your Twitterdom comes equipped with a giant megaphone, and anyone in earshot can hear what you have to say. Not only that, but anyone *not* in earshot can also be the recipient of your message, limited only by your knowledge of their @username and whether or not they actually pay attention to their @-messages. It is a brilliant platform for the genes to kick in, grab their own voice, and start creating Your Brand and your bravado. This is not a bad thing in all cases, only where the genes are sculpting away, chiseling out characteristics in your virtual profile to create a person who is not your True Self.

For the people who are using Twitter to become more authentic, genuinely – more power to you. I challenge you to examine your own behaviors to see if *you* are leading the way, or if your genetic impulses have a say in your tweets. The rest of us will just camp out on the highest vantage point in our own Twitterdoms, and brace for the next fusillade (thanks Daniel Pink, that word is fun on my skin) of data from @breakingnews.

The secret life of tweets is also genetically driven, for each message (albeit unconsciously, as tweets don't have a conscious or a conscience) has the inherent potential to become The Next Great Retweet, illuminating the world with its sparkling 140 characters or less. Though the ideas themselves may be blissfully unaware, those who tweet are cautiously in tune with the retweetability factor, another force that may genetically taint the authenticity of a message when it is created. (Unless, of course, you're simply passing along the Hot Potato of Seemingly Useful Digital Information.)

In either case, the genes are the shadow government, planting information and disinformation into the ranks of the Tweetinista. Their urge is to cry out, in the guise and clothing of Braveheart: "Look at me! I'm interesting, and I know stuff! I am strong and cultured and can kick your butt if I need to! Look at my tall hill, from whence I can see the entire land!"

Now I'm certainly not suggesting that everyone's genes run their own personal show. Some souls, like @stevewhitaker, seem to simply be using the platform to blow off some intensely entertaining non-sequitur steam. (But the way he tweets, sometimes I do wonder if the guy is just trying to get laid – either digitally or realistically – and that would surely reflect the genes cranking into their memetic action.)

Tractor trailer crashed into the vitamin section at Integral Yoga in #cville
11:52AM on 6/16/2010 from paper-journal

Mihaly's second veil, after Genes, is Culture. He explains that we are all both consciously and subconsciously programmed by the perceived notion of what is "right" in our environment, as well as the customs and expectations of those around us. Is the "you" that you've come to define really part of your Self, or is it part of what your culture is suggesting should be part of your Self? It's a subtle distinction that requires asking the question, over and over again: "What's your motivation?"

> "Excessive acculturation leads one to see reality only through the veils of the culture. A person who invests psychic energy exclusively in goals prescribed by society is forfeiting the possibility of choice…
>
> It is dangerous to take too seriously the picture of the world as painted by one's culture. First, to do so limits the scope of any individual potential."
>
> Csikszentmihalyi, *The Evolving Self*, p. 72-73

I had some difficulty trying to figure out how the veil of culture could be inhibiting my pursuit of authenticity through Twitter. But then, I realized, it's not necessarily *me* that's inhibited, it's the whole medium. There is no way you *can't* embed cultural assumptions in the limited space allotted for a tweet. And, like I mentioned a couple weeks ago when I started reading the news from the *actual newspaper* that gets delivered to our house every morning, the "ordinary news" is almost always missing on Twitter. It's just not "worthy enough" to be highlighted and passed on:

> "It is liberating to question the descriptions of reality of one's culture, and especially those presented by the media. As one opens up the newspaper in the morning, it is well to remember that what one reads represents a necessarily biased view…

> It is also occasionally useful to take off the distorting glasses that we have grown accustomed to wearing, and look at what is happening from a different perspective. To what extent here I have accepted other people's definition of who I am and what I could be?"
>
> Csikszentmihalyi, *The Evolving Self*, p. 77

Am I tweeting regularly, and updating Facebook, and living in my Inbox, and digitally breadcrumbing my day because my culture believes this is what I *should* be doing? (My intuition tells me that, personally, I'm not so entrenched by this veil. And yet I still go through the motions, almost instinctively.) But the next topic is not just a veil; it's a productivity killer as well.

> I really do enjoy writing at @getopenspace, partly bc of the coffee, partly bc of the lime green decor
> 12:42PM on 6/16/2010 from paper-journal

The final veil is simultaneously a provider of illusions *and* a productivity/gumption block: Ego. Perhaps it is the illusions themselves that do the blocking. Pirsig says that the remedies for ego as a productivity killer are modesty, skepticism, and openness to possibilities. All of these require a self-reflective consciousness, a way of being that makes us stop and think about what we're doing and feeling and why, and gives us the opportunity to continually improve ourselves.

Realization: One of the goals of continuous improvement of the Self is to get us in touch with our own authenticity – a precursor to achieving flow in how we do things, and an enabler for *doing* things that result in high quality outcomes.

> "Once the mind realized its autonomy, individuals were able to conceive of themselves as independent agents with their own self-interest. For the first time, it was possible for people to emancipate themselves from the

rule of genes and of culture. A person could now have unique dreams, and take an individual stance based on personal goals.

While the self brought the gift of personal freedom, it also spun another veil, as thick as the two earlier ones: the illusions of the ego."

Csikszentmihalyi, *The Evolving Self*, p. 77

The ego is, simply, the symbols that represent who you think you are. For a lot of people, these symbols are material: your house, your car, your furniture. You may define yourself in terms of the number of times you tweet per day, or maybe even in the totality of the persona you project online. The symbols can be tied to people: your spouse, your family, your kids, your pets. Symbols of the ego can also be personal characteristics, for example if you define yourself by your style of clothing, or your super-cool shoes, or your wild mane of purple hair.

I used to have purple hair (more than half my life ago). Although it only lasted for a couple of weeks, at that time a couple of weeks was a substantial fraction of my life span, and the experiment was an interesting dance of ego intertwined with self. Ego said "Look at me! I'm different, and interesting, and I'd like you to validate that!" Self, much more genuine and demure, did not need to be noticed or validated. Self was just fulfilled by the courageousness of getting the purple hair in the first place, openly cutting through the heavy veil of culture.

I think a lot of relationships fall prey to this dichotomy as well. You meet someone, you really like them, and then all of a sudden your ego is shouting "Look at how fun and likeable I am! I have no mental or emotional issues! I want you to like me too, and I need some constant validation because I get hungry for approval a few times a day!" Meanwhile, the Self is hanging out on the couch, comfortable and chilled out as it always is – because it innately recognizes its own value and is satisfied with that. "Hey Ego, will you pipe down? I'm trying to relax over here, and enjoy the tapestry of life and experience it moment by moment, and with all your needy whimpering, you're chasing away all the butterflies. Cut it out."

Ego gets in the way of *just being*:

> "It is for this reason that religious and philosophical systems here always have been so ambivalent about material stirrings, and prescribed instead the development of a self that has a value independent of external accomplishments...
>
> Unfortunately the temptation to use other people to aggrandize the ego is also quite strong, and many people find it difficult to resist. Parents who are overprotective of their children, lovers who are exceedingly jealous, paternalistic employers... often do not care much for the well-being of the people with whom they interact...
>
> If a person refuses to invest psychic energy in goals, gives up desires, and does not identify with any idea, belief, object, or human relationship, then in a certain sense he or she becomes invulnerable. By our nature we want certain things to happen; when our desires are frustrated, we suffer. By giving up expectation and desire – in effect, by giving up the self – one can no longer be frustrated."
> Csikszentmihalyi, *The Evolving Self*, p. 80-81

I have a lot of heartburn with some of these ideas, even though their utility and relevance resonates with me. *It is because of this heartburn that I know the veil of ego still covers me.*

I'll undoubtedly revisit this passage later as I untangle and peel back the layers of my ego. But my reaction right now is as follows. If giving up expectations and desires essentially means giving up the self, then wouldn't it be better overall to *deal with* the frustrations of unmet desire, and yet still live soulfully and authentically? I'll have to cook that one in my mind for a while.

> Seeking to snap out of a little ADT. Wow, that grapefruit guarana @getopenspace is pretty nice.
> 1:49PM on 6/16/2010 from paper-journal

Mihaly is not the only guy who has explored the veils of illusion that color our perceptions and experiences. The concept of the *seven veils* is also deeply rooted in myth and tradition, symbolizing the systematic shedding of productivity blocks on the path to self-realization and a deeper, more soulful experience of spirituality. Tom Robbins fictionalized the process of cutting through the layers of illusion in *Skinny Legs and All*, in such an exquisitely articulate and salacious manner that I won't even tarnish its Joycean elegance with my comments. The veils that Robbins explains are a little more finely grained than Mihaly's, but they all align. But if Robbins had been sitting at my dining room table that morning with Pirsig and Mihaly, he would not have wasted his time in wise contemplation of the lessons that I was uncovering. He would not have admired the process, or compared notes with the other philosophers of modern life, or offered his sage advice and otherworldly commentary – he'd probably just be handing out the literary LSD.

Seven Veils	**Veils of Maya**	**Manifested in:**
1 gender	genes	sexism
2 race	genes	racism
3 class	culture	class struggle
4 culture	culture	ethnocentrism
5 age/time	ego	age discrimination
6 belief/religion	ego	fanaticism
7 conduct	ego	behaviorism

Usually hate custom ringtones, but impressed with that
guy's Super Mario jingle
2:21PM on 6/16/2010 from paper-journal

I keep asking the question "What's your motivation?" – and it
would be appropriate for me to answer that question about
Project Disconnected and my journaling experience. It's a different engagement than blogging or posting on Twitter or
Facebook, for sure, mostly due to the lack of self-censorship. If
anyone reads this journal and thinks it's utterly stupid and not
worth the paper it's printed on, I fully respect that. I'm not writing this for you. I'm writing this for the person who wants to live
a productive, authentic, engaging life in which technology helps
them transcend boundaries, develop their sense of Self, and
make a difference – whatever difference is *meaningful to them.*

I'm writing for the person who wastes too much time online,
and feels kinda bad about it (but maybe not bad enough to
change behavior), who senses that there must be a different
way to live (but can't fathom what it might possibly be). I'm
writing for the person who has become so embedded in the
virtual life that the real one just doesn't seem as vibrant any
more. I don't want you to miss out. *I don't want to miss out*
(any more).

So what's my motivation? I want to help people uncover better
relationships with their technologies and their social media, a
better sense of Self (and sense of the soul) online, and an actionable way to balance the real and virtual worlds. Why? So you
can stay in the here and now – the moment – *by knowing where
the moment actually is,* and how to find it. I want to help *myself*
accomplish this first. I am not writing this journal right now *so
that* it will eventually become a book, although I sense that it
will. I am writing it because the *process* of touching the emerging
words with this pen is drawing out insights from the twinkling

illusions, shattering veils, and unblocking those invisible boulders that have been impeding my personal path for years.

It's time to go find Tracey's gold Volvo
4:57PM on 6/16/2010 from paper-journal

6/17/2010 (Thursday)

It's now Day 17 or Day 18 of the experiment, depending upon whether you're a zero-based counter or not. I may have encountered the Something Entirely Unexpected last night, but I'm not completely sure, so I'll see if it happens again before I commit it to paper. In the meantime, I'll continue my sordid relationship with Oolong tea, because I'm really enjoying the break from the ordinary, as well as the momentary descent into the sweet dusky abyss of the non-coffee genre.

> Sea turtle videos itself in Caribbean: http://www.youtube.com/watch?v=E43sg-Ytt58
> 8:03AM on 6/17/2010 from paper-journal

> Hypnotist worked: escaped dentist office teeth cleaning without panic attack (this time)
> 12:21PM on 6/17/2010 from paper-journal

Before I can move on, it's now time for me to go back and revisit the saga of the sleep doctor. A couple weeks ago I recounted the story of my intense postpartum insomnia, my foray into the madness of sleeping no more than an hour and a half at a time for nearly three years. It was both painful and instructive, as pain *should* be, and taught me that it's possible to make constructive use of all 24 hours in a day (even if a large fraction of those are spent playing Texas Hold 'Em online, jockeying for a higher payoff from a tournament win). Eventually, the pattern became destructive. The hallucinations just refused to go away, I had burnt hundreds of English muffins and other starchy artifacts accidentally left in the toaster, and I was running out of productive work to keep me occupied. I was also running out of strategies for bluffing my state of awakeness while semi-conscious. It was all mixed up together in one very unhealthy, cortisol-laden existence.

And then I discovered Ambien. The courtship is not really that relevant; the breakup, however, is. When I went in for my appointment to get a new fix, the physician was coolly unsympathetic, a Robin Williams of family practice: "That stuff rots your brain. You're too young! I only let my older patients rot their brains. They only have a couple decades left, anyways. But go see Chris... he'll help you."

I got a little psyched thinking that maybe my doctor was tipping me off to a hookup on the street. No such luck, though. When I called the number that my doctor had scribbled on the 2x2 inch shard ripped off the top of his white lunch bag, I was greeted with the southern charm of a woman who'd certainly woken up cheerful and well-rested that morning: "Neurology and sleep medicine... how may I help you?"

"Uhmmm, yeah..." I said. Three second pause. "I need help."

"You need a sleep consultation?" I guess my tone was more information rich than the two-page medical history that might have been requested next. My desperation hung like a wet towel in the heavy air of the stilted conversation, so my appointment was set for the next day.

I think I was expecting a little voodoo, or Timothy Leary, or maybe something in between. But the good sleep doctor, a guy my age who looked like he had biked into work and just thrown a white lab coat over his biker Spandex, got to the root cause of my problem in a matter of minutes. "Oh yeah," he said. "Your body just got in the habit of waking itself up every time you were *really* getting close to falling into a deep sleep. We can fix that."

Victory! He's got something even more potent than Ambien, something that won't rot my brain. I felt giddy, invigorated, *saved* – until he gave me a few sheets of instructions on how we were gonna use this "behavioral sleep therapy" thing to crack my insomnia habit. "21 days is all it takes", he told me. "But about 17 days into it, you're going to start cussing me and think this was the stupidest idea ever. Don't let your anger run the show… just give it a few days after that."

The protocol was straightforward: 1) Don't go to bed until after midnight, and not until you're ready to fall asleep… even if it's 3am, or 5am, or later. 2) Wake up at 7am. Get out of bed… get moving… start your day. No excuses. 3) No naps. The first week was easy, with bedtime at 3am or 4am and wake-up promptly at 7am. I was invigorated! For the first time in many moons I could sleep longer than an hour and a half, and my body was thanking me already.

Then came the second week, and with it a little more tension. Bedtime crept backwards, first at 2am, then at 1am. I was still waking up between three and five times a night in the midst of my newly discovered skill of achieving rest.

On Day 17, I transformed. It was as if the skin on level-headed me had been unzipped, pulled back, and a sailor stepped out. Not just any sailor, mind you – but a pirate – and a pirate whose ship had just been hijacked, maniacally drifting in twenty foot waves of confusion, with all the right language to express how much this crack behavioral sleep program was NOT working! That $%!*& doctor! @(^^%$ insomnia! What a waste of my #%!@$% time! Where's my Ambien?

Day 18: $!&((*#&&!%*!@@!!!!!!!!!

On Day 19 I slept for nine hours straight, for the first time in my emerging state of rested existence.

By Day 21, I had established a new pattern. It's now been mine for two years, and although I still go through periodic bouts of insomnia even today, I can usually trace the disquiet to something I'm actually worrying about or working on busily. So it's *normal people* insomnia, not that demonic possession style insomnia that rattles your cage, and that's cool with me.

The Something Completely Unexpected in my behavioral sleep therapy was biphasic: first, the meltdown that I reached on Day 17, followed by the utter calm experienced by Day 21. In trying to figure out what my Day 17 experience was for Project Disconnected, I surveyed a whole host of thoughts. Do you think spontaneously reverting to old habits like trying to click through to Facebook on my Droid counts as aberrant behavior... as my *something unexpected*? How about convincing myself that it's not cheating if I go to one person's Facebook page directly and just don't check new status updates? Or what about doing Google searches on a person just so you can see, through search, what their latest Google Chat or Google Buzz statuses were? Oh, the sickness, the attention devoted to all the possible ways one can circumvent one's own Rules of Engagement.

Or maybe it's just the 15 minutes I spent this morning cussing at my stupid computer, and this stupid waste of time called Project Disconnected, because it's not working! I don't feel any more whole, or well rounded, or more balanced, or insightful, or anything! And look at all the trivia I've missed out on over the past three weeks.

But I'm now becoming attracted to figuring out what sorts of contributions I can make to the world. My attention is turning to focus on the universe beyond the cobwebs and the veils, be-yond the forces that get in the way of doing something useful – those mysterious forces that obstruct even water and air. There *has* been a shift in me, but it's just not entirely what I expected. The cobwebs and veils are being ceremoniously lifted from ev-ery *other* aspect of my life, not just the part I'm living in the vir-tual, and I should probably admit that this is a lot more internal work than I'd bargained for.

> Lots of tornadoes today in ND&MN! http://www.spc.noaa.gov/climo/online
> 7:09PM on 6/17/2010 from paper-journal

This has been a rather time-warped week. Whereas the past few weeks have labored on with 36 to 48 hour days, where I can't move forward productively with any of those hours, this week has had 1) normal length days, 2) all of them have been expe-rienced in the order they fall on my calendar, and 3) the hours have been simultaneously long enough to engage in, and short enough to float by effortlessly.

What is *most* revealing is that I haven't even been doing anything that might be considered *fun*. I've been working, and writing, and cleaning house, and doing laundry, and packing for my trip, and cleaning out closets. There are only two things that have distin-guished this past week from those that have come before: 1) I have been actively busting through productivity traps with the appropriate remedies, including slicing, and 2) I've managed to get into *flow* at least once a day. I haven't even had to slice that much – the slices come more naturally now, the knife so much sharper once the steely productivity traps are loosed from your bloody leg.

Realization: Email is like a pot of water on the stove. New messages that you'd really like to read only come in when you're *not watching the Inbox*. A watched Inbox never boils.

The message of Day 17, if I'm reading and interpreting it properly, is the paradox of *technological hopelessness*. I don't want to give up the technology and the social media, because part of what it enables is part of me. But the whole socio-technical system seems like it's wandering around in the desert, seeking a drop of soul, a way to balance the joy and the nonsense to bring sustenance to being. Pirsig says you just have to *care* about what you're doing, and I'm sure by that he meant veil-free care:

> "If the problem of technological hopelessness is caused by the absence of care, both by technologists and anti-technologists; and if care and Quality are external and internal aspects of the same thing, then it follows logically that what really causes technological hopelessness is absence of the perception of Quality in technology by both technologists and antitechnologists."
>
> Pirsig, *Zen and the Art of Motorcycle Maintenance*, p. 282

This is a pretty heavy passage with lots of long, repeating words. What does it mean? To me (and it might mean something entirely different to you, I recognize), I've got to refer to my favorite definition of quality first, which comes from ISO 8402. (Now, since I spent so many years *thinking* about the issue of quality in PhD school, I have encountered my fair share of definitions of quality, and thus feel well qualified to pick a favorite.) ISO 8402 says quality is "the totality of features and characteristics of an entity that bear on its ability to satisfy stated and implied needs."

To have quality, then, you first need an *entity*. This can be a product, service, object, animal, vegetable, mineral, concept, person, or relationship. The entity can probably be many other things too. Second, that entity needs to *do something for another entity*. (Why two entities? Doesn't that just make it more complicated? No. That other entity is the one that *has* the needs.)

I'm using the word "needs" here very loosely too, decoupled from the concepts of needs and desires and their relationship to suffering, a la Ram Dass and Mihaly. Come to think of it, I should invite Ram Dass to the next imaginary breakfast conversation at my dining room table. It would especially be a trip to see if he could get Tom Robbins to open up and chat.)

So an entity has to *do* something for another entity for that *first* entity to qualify for the privilege of *having quality*. Not having *good* quality, but the ability to be considered as having any manifestation of quality at all. It's kind of like if we said something must have *energy* to have a temperature. An idea or concept, for example, doesn't have a temperature because it's not composed of physical stuff, atomic and subatomic particles, moving around with energy. But if that idea or concept can inspire, motivate, or *hang up* an individual, causing them productivity blocks and maybe even draping veils over their perception, then that idea definitely has *quality*. And notice that the quality will be perceived far differently by the person who was inspired, versus the person who was hurt, inhibited, or held back.

The element of *care* that vaporizes technological hopelessness is associated with how an entity meets the implied needs. *Implied* indicates *unspoken*: either the need is so obvious that it's not discussed, or it's hidden below the surface — the entity that has the needs hasn't realized it has them yet, or maybe it knows what its needs are, but it just can't vocalize or communicate them. Either way, it's going to take a lot of *care* and consideration on the part of the craftsman to reach and get in that second entity's head (or whatever the "head equivalent" is for that particular entity).

In your Twitterdom, the developers who run the site have addressed the stated needs: to provide a way for people to communicate with each other, singly or en masse, in 140 characters or less. The implied needs depend entirely on what you *think* you want to get out of the system and your interactions with it. It's personal to you, and so you're going to have to be the one that uncovers those implied needs, otherwise you risk technological hopelessness by your own hand. So too if you let the veils convince you that they're smarter than you, and you let the veils decide what your implied needs are on your behalf. Bottom line: quality is shut out, soulfulness is punctuated, technological hopelessness spreads – unless you can authentically identify your implied needs.

I think this is the identical phenomenon that's going on right now in the Facebook security debate, concerning the massive concerns about the privacy of personal information and the responses in the popular media that have followed. People are beginning to taste the technological hopelessness that can emerge when implied needs are left unsatisfied. Luster is lacked, quality is eroded, tastes become acrid; pioneers set off to explore new territory to soothe their shattered souls.

> Five days from now I'll be at the wonderful @raskassas in Boulder… ahhh
> 9:51PM on 6/17/2010 from paper-journal

6/18/2010 (Friday)

This was one of those mornings that I'd yearned for in March...
sipping Oolong tea on the deck, the breeze that perfect shade of
just-cool that's in total equilibrium with your body temperature,
the deep blue of the sky hovering over the city buildings in anticipation of solar progress. It was a yearning that I felt then, but
today, it's more of a quiet enjoyment. I'm learning to soak up the
things that renew my spirit so I can be just as content during the
long winter.

> Heading out on a 3mi trek to the Corner and back
> 11:27AM on 6/18/2010 from paper-journal

> Littlejohn's mushroom melt, Pellegrino, & 2.75mi
> 1:17PM on 6/18/2010 from paper-journal

One thing I really enjoy about walking in areas where there are
a lot of people is, and I know this is somewhat cliché, but... *people watching*. And people *overhearing*. Some of it is mildly irritant
and abrasive, like the guy on the motorcycle who thinks it's a
public service to share his Ozzy CD with everyone on his route.
Today there was also a mother and her 3 year old girl walking
along the brick sidewalk flanking the University of Virginia. The
girl asked if she was going to get a treat on their trip.

"I doubt it," said the mother.

"But Mommy, I've forgotten what 'doubt it' means," the tiny girl
replied.

The mother was not rattled by this eloquently executed device of toddler literary manipulation. "Probably not," the mother said, explaining the notion of doubt.

"No, *no*... I *really did* forget what it means!" the girl innocently replied.

> 78min til my next haircut
> 1:42PM on 6/18/2010 from paper-journal

My thoughts over the past two days have been in an entirely different place than the past several weeks, and I'm sensing that technological detox is indeed the impetus for bringing me to where I am now. No longer do I feel overwhelmed by information, plagued by trivia, possessed by "waiting for something to happen," or driven by the thoughts and activities of my social network. I'm not lamenting missed opportunities, wondering what other people are doing, getting sad about what *I haven't thought about doing*, or living vicariously through any other mechanism than my own eyes, and ears, and here-and-now senses. As a result, my productivity is now reasonable – not amazing, but reasonable – I'm getting things done, piece by piece, slice by slice, without a sense of dread or uncommon gravity. And my thoughts have turned to *what I might like to pursue next* – what sorts of things spin my heart, get me excited, and can make a positive difference for other people! It's a "sea change" of sorts, the kind you might expect after sailing in an icy Hudson Bay for months, and then find yourself mysteriously transported to the middle of the tropical part of the Indian Ocean. You might need a bigger boat.

Realization: Battery life on your Droid is remarkably and noticeably improved when you're not clicking on the thing 530+ times a day.

> It's Walkalajara night... in 10 more min
> 6:10PM on 6/18/2010 from paper-journal

"The world in which we live constantly bombards us with messages and information. In a study called *How Much Information? 2009: Report on American Consumers*, the Global Information Industry Center at the University of California, San Diego, indicates that Americans spend a considerable amount of time receiving information, an average of 11.8 hours a day.

Imagine that – the average American spends almost twelve hours per day at home receiving information through television, newspapers, magazines, email, ezines, Facebook, Twitter, websites, movies, and a plethora of other sources. We are barraged with messages, and thus communicating is becoming a little like trying to whisper in a crowded room – there is so much noise that it is hard to get the attention of anyone.

As we find ourselves flooded with statistics, news and opinions, it becomes harder to filter through the noise and evaluate what is truly important. It seems that we are more challenged than ever to balance this steady stream of information with equal portions of thoughtfulness and reflection."

Stuart Lord, *Naropa Magazine* (Spring 2010), p. 1

Realization: I had always thought my time surfing online *was* my quiet period of thoughtfulness and reflection – my "relaxing" time. Now, I'm wondering if that wasn't just the veil of culture obfuscating my underlying *real* needs. (And in particular, that one very important need of connecting with Self, so that the cobwebs can untangle and the veils can lift, and you can actually start *getting somewhere* that feels right.)

I finished reading Daniel Pink's book *Drive* over the past two days as well. This book asks the question: How do you tap into that really pure motivation, that *drive*, which propels you into a state of flow? He characterizes three types of motivation: 1) the "stick," where you're motivated to because there's a *penalty* if you don't, 2) the "carrot," where you're motivated because you *get* something if you complete a task or achieve a goal, and 3) the "third drive," where you do something because you're just genuinely, authentically interested in doing it. Penalties are irrelevant in this third case, and bonuses and rewards become merely incidental.

The underlying theme that's been heavy in my mind since my focus shifted from barriers to opportunities is hinted at in *Drive*, but never outright acknowledged. And that is: the struggle of *authenticity vs. duty*. Carrots and sticks seem to *create* a duty even where there is none. In other cases, duty is created by a veil. In particular, culture and ego can set up either real duties or perceptions of duties. For example, you may have a duty to go to work each day because ego tells you that you need to uphold your image as a solid breadwinner for your family. Conversely, you may head to work each day because you just love the environment, the people, and the things you do – and this is you operating out of a sense of authenticity.

But do not forget: carrots and sticks are both illusions of culture, except when encountered in nature (e.g. in a garden).

Sometimes, you think that your real self *wants* a duty. But when you invite that duty into your life, you can discover that it's just the script that your ego or your culture has set into place in your being that made you *think* you wanted that duty, and so you become disillusioned. Both *duty* and the *perception of duty* are at odds, in many cases, with the pursuit and achievement of authenticity. That's the point, really – if you authentically feel that something is *not* a duty or obligation, and yet you *still* want to do it, that's the secret potion for enjoying yourself, becoming more authentic, and even achieving flow.

"Everything will be OK in the end. If it's not OK, it's not the end." -unknown
9:29PM on 6/18/2010 from paper-journal

Yet I do have one regret today concerning my self-imposed exile from Facebook. I would love to get online and wish my friend Tricia McCanna (aka Dee Dee Lee) a happy 35th birthday. But indeed, I'll take the high road and resist, since it's not permissible under my current Rules of Engagement. Well, Tricia, just know that I'm thinking about you, hoping that you and your family celebrate your birthday in the most excellent of ways, and actually – the fact that my birthday wish to you will now be immortalized in print could make it just a tiny little bit better than if you just saw it scroll by on Facebook one day :)

6/19/2010 (Saturday)

Yahoo Headlines this morning featured this title: "10 Wackiest Attractions in America." My first thought: "Cool! One of them *has* to be Carhenge!" And indeed it was. Carhenge is a little 2-acre park off the side of the road a couple miles north of Alliance, Nebraska. In the late 1980's, this one guy decided he was going to build a replica of Stonehenge on his dad's farm, only instead of using giant rocks, he'd use old junker cars painted navy gray. The result: a roadside attraction that I've ceremoniously introduced to several handfuls of people. It was easy to do; there were a couple years in the late 1990's where I often drove from Colorado to South Dakota and back, and you can either be enchanted by the vast nothingness of Lusk or Lost Springs, Wyoming, or take the scenic route by Carhenge and thus appreciate the local arts and culture. The edifice is entertaining not so much for its art (although that's fun too), but for its *unexpectedness*. I mean, who *really* expects to see Stonehenge burst forth from the wild bar-renness of a sandy, western Nebraska wheat field?

> I've been really enjoying the word "fumaroles" today, and the way it rolls out of my mouth
> 12:51PM on 6/19/2010 from paper-journal

Today has been a day of transition. I really haven't felt the urge to be online. I haven't even felt the urge to think about whether I *am* or *am not* online. What a difference! I don't think I've lived this way for at least 5 or 10 years.

> It's always a great day when you have to buy a smaller bathing suit.
> 6:36PM on 6/19/2010 from paper-journal

Todd, Alex and I are hanging with Lead Man Larry at Dürty Nelly's
8:01PM on 6/19/2010 from paper-journal

Say you'll come back when you can
Whenever your airplane happens to land
Maybe I'll be here back too
It all depends on what's with you

Hung up waiting for a windy day
Kite on ice since the first of February
Mama Bee saying that the wind might blow
But standin here I say I just don't know

New ones comin as the old ones go
Everything's moving here but much too slowly
Little bit quicker and we might have time
To say 'how do you do?' before we're left behind"
Jerry Garcia & Robert Hunter, *Cosmic Charlie*

6/20/2010 (Sunday)

At the #firstwednesdays gathering a couple of weeks ago, I recall talking to one of the techie guys there about my project to
disconnect from social and other media and see what happens.
"Oh!" he said, in instant recognition. "You mean like a Digital
Sabbath, only longer, like Lent." Since then, I've not awakened
on a Sunday without thinking "today's the Digital Sabbath."
Apparently, he was referring to a practice that's picking up lately,
whereby a person will choose a day of the week and entirely
eschew all connectivity for that day, declaring it their electronic
day of rest. "I've been doing that for a couple years already,"
commented @rduplain, ever the trendsetter.

> I can't believe it's already SPIE time. Must finish packing and
> washing today.
> 10:13AM on 6/20/2010 from paper-journal

I mentioned that yesterday seemed to be a day of transition,
and today, I'm figuring out why. I am uniquely able, today, to step
outside of the jittery tiger-in-a-box that I've been for a little
too long, and to calmly and objectively reflect on the churning,
confusing, ugly feelings that my relationship with my virtual me
has been promoting. The ugliness that I've been thinking about
this morning is *why in the world I'd be jealous or envious* of people
who seem to be having more fun and fulfillment than me online,
as evidenced by their intriguing and engaging Facebook status
updates. So what that it's all part of the illusion anyway, and it's
just as easy for me to post tales of fulfillment as it is for the next
guy, and it's immaterial whether those tales are tall or short. The
message is clear, to me, and it's part of *my* illusion: you're having

more fun and a more enjoyable time than me, and I just suck because I can't think of anything to do. What can I do to get rid of these ugly feelings?

> "Still we have to find a way to live with our disturbing feelings, such as jealousy and envy. These emotions can be so sickening and corrosive that we don't want to leave them raw, wallowing in them for years and getting nowhere with them. But what can we do short of trying to get rid of them? A clue is to be found in the very distaste we feel for them: anything so difficult to accept must have a special kind of shadow in it, a germ of creativity shrouded in a veil of repulsion.
>
> As we have so often found, in matters of the soul the most unworthy pieces turn out to be the most creative. The stone the builders reject becomes the cornerstone.
>
> Both envy and jealousy are common experiences. Either emotion can make a person feel ugly. There is nothing noble in either of them. At the same time, a person may feel oddly attached to them.
>
> Mythology suggests that both envy and jealousy are rooted deeply in the soul. Even the gods become jealous."
>
> Thomas Moore, *Care of the Soul*, p. 83

Now, granted, delving into the world of archetypal envy and jealousy may seem to be a heavy-handed approach to understanding aspects of my technology addiction. But bear with me here. I think by embellishing the tension, something harmonious and useful might just pop out of the strings, at least eventually.

If the ancient gods were challenged by these dark and gangrenous feelings, then I should be *honored* to work through their lessons through my technology issues. I am a cog in a machine thousands of years old, and no matter how putrescent the oil that greases its tiny interconnected parts, I am an ingredient in the turn of the Big Wheel. It's even ugly just admitting that I've felt this way.

Although there is nothing noble in the feelings themselves, there is a certain regality concerning the process of working through them. And if Thomas Moore says there's a hidden gem in the experience of these emotions, I'll go with his intuition. After all, he is a *soul expert*, and I *need me some of that*.

> "The only way *out* of jealousy is *through* it. We may have to let jealousy have its way with us and do its job of re-orienting fundamental values. Its pain comes, at least in part, from opening up to unexplored territory and letting go of old, familiar truths in the face of unknown and threatening new possibilities."
>
> Thomas Moore, *Care of the Soul*, p. 87

Moore reveals that, in his study of jealousy and envy as a therapist, he has indeed discovered some remedies. First of all, jealousy is an indication that you're *not getting enough of something you think you need*. Furthermore, you might perceive that someone else *is* getting it, which will interject the perception that other people are influencing or causing your jealousy (even though they're just incidental to *your* experience of that feeling). So according to Moore, I'm not getting enough of something I think I need. Two options here: 1) I can go get more of what I think I need, as long as it doesn't become my "insatiable tape," or 2) I can eliminate the need itself, or my perception that I have the need. As a prerequisite, I've got to figure out *what I think I need more of*. That's gonna be the tough part.

There are simple remedies for envy, too, it turns out. Moore says you shouldn't merely try to *get rid* of it, but to use its instructive qualities in the same way you might make use of pain:

> "It makes us stop and take notice of something that has gone wrong and needs attention. What has gone is that our close-up vision has been blurred. Envy is hyperopia of the soul, an inability to see what is closest to us. We fail to see the necessity and value in our own lives."
>
> Thomas Moore, *Care of the Soul*, p. 87

If I mash up these two ideas, I might find a path through *both* conflated feelings. (A ha! Now I get to *use* that clandestine C-word!) I need more of *seeing what is closest to me*, and *more recognition* of the necessity and value of my own life. Thank goodness I ran across James Park in a random Google search, because his unorthodox, brazen and scintillating treatise on jealousy in romantic relationships has something to say (rather surprisingly) about how I can forge a healthier relationship with my online streams of information!

We're about to go on a ridiculously grand diversion here, akin to dropping by Tierra del Fuego en route from the east coast of the United States to a village in Bhutan. The southernmost place in the non-Antarctic world is a place of extremes and simplicity, as we'll soon find. Before we go there, though, I've got to convince you that the human-computer or human-online relationship is *entirely* a human relationship. And ever more fortunately, I don't have to convince you myself, because Byron Reeves and Clifford Nass have been studying this for years, and their arguments are far more compelling than mine might ever be. They have found, through their research, that people treat computers and new media *as if they were other people*.

> "Our strategy for learning about media was to go to the social science section of the library, find theories and experiments about human-*human* interaction – and then borrow. We did the same for information about how people respond to the natural environment, borrowing freely. Take out a pen, cross out 'human' or

'environment,' and substitute *media*. When we did this, all of the predictions and experiments led to the media equation: people's responses to media are fundamentally social and natural.

Media experiences equal human experiences...

People's responses show that media are more than just tools. Media are treated politely, they can invade our body space, they can have personalities that match our own, they can be a teammate, and they can elicit gender stereotypes. Media can evoke emotional responses, *demand attention, threaten us*, influence memories, and change ideas of what is natural. Media are full participants in our social and natural world."

Reeves & Nass, *The Media Equation*, p. 251

Your virtual life is, then, the brilliant result of a geological anthropomorphism, formed and crafted by the heat and pressure of frequent and intensive social interactions in the digital medium. Over time, your tools and the real world people behind them amalgamate, and then blend into that singular persona that you interact with online. A postmodern, McLuhanesque state of being emerges, in which the medium is *not only* the message, but the *relationship* as well. All of those emotions crop up in the whitespace between you and the things that you do in your virtual world.

So we're in South America, almost to Patagonia, and the landscape is becoming ever more stark and pointed. Your relationship with the online world is about to undergo a little counseling, but first, you have to become totally silent and comfortable in the brisk chill and bright expanse of this uncommon end of the Earth.

Kudos to @jeffgunther for your cameo on p.85-88 of Pink's book Drive. Go #cville!

2:01PM on 6/20/2010 from paper-journal

Enter James Park, our counselor (and how appropriate too, in the setting of an imagined national park, a namesake). He is not a therapist or counselor by profession, but a scholar of divinity and indie author extraordinaire, whose insights are as striking and thought-provoking as the landscape. He is in the business of reframing ideas to blow away antiquated mental models.

As a self-described existential philosopher, he has also devised some viewpoints on jealousy and how to overcome it.

"Jealousy arises in human relationships because of comparison, competition, and fear of being replaced. We can easily see why jealousy often arises in relationships that involve only our physical and psychological dimensions — because comparison and competition are almost unavoidable when we think of people in terms of their bodies and personalities. But if we become more Authentic, we move beyond jealousy because we love from the depths of our self-creating uniqueness...

But becoming 'better' than others really means being *the same*. *Excellence* is a measure of *conformity* to an agreed cultural ideal. Jealousy is prevented not be excellence but by *irreplaceability*."

James Park, *New Ways of Loving*, Chapter 5

The virtual world is a petri dish of potential jealousy for the "normal" person, the person who's still susceptible to Ego, and Boredom, and Anxiety, and Impatience. You *know* your friends are comparing your status updates with your other friends, making subjective value judgments all the while, culling out who's normal from who's "got problems." You know (especially those of you who might still be in high school or college) that there's an underlying theme of competition to establish your domain, reputation and position. And fear of being replaced? Well, even though I didn't think this would ever impact me – I admit feeling pangs of unknowingness the last two times I became aware of someone "unfriending" me. Clearly they could not allow me in their quota of allowable friends – despite the fact that I'm not even one of those challenged people who's stuck on Farmville or Vampire Wars or the latest irritation of the week! I am unlike all those people who clearly do not have enough to do with their time :) – and yet I still get unfriended.

Like Thomas Moore, James Park has a very simple remedy for overcoming jealousy: to become unique and irreplaceable as an individual so that there is no need for anyone to compare you to others or engage in a competition. It sounds brilliantly simple, and it is!

> "If we consistently pursue our new invented life-purposes, after several years of growth, we might re-invent ourselves. From an existential perspective, we *are* what we pursue; we can be understood by the *projects* we undertake...
>
> We will become: one of a kind, singular, irreplaceable, inimitable, incomparable, unprecedented...
>
> Not only can we become unrepeatable persons by reorganizing our lives Authentically, but we can create unique ways of becoming unique!"

> James Park, *New Ways of Loving*, Chapter 5

Let's see if we can sum this up:

Who	**Source of Jealousy**	**Remedy**
Moore	Your needs or desires are not being met; you require more time with something	Reorient values to see what's closest the to you; go *through* the jealousy; eliminate needs or desires
Park	Comparison Competition Fear of being replaced	Work on becoming uniquely, authentically you! Cultivate your *Self*! (Note: this approach is highly conducive to achieving flow as well!)

Like I said, it was necessary to take a scenic detour into embellishment to be able to banish jealousy and envy from lurking deep in the virtual soul. The remedy for disengaging from these distracting feelings can be blended together from the elixirs that we've collected:

1) Understand what you think you need more of, and either get it, or eliminate the need or desire for it.
2) Spend time seeing, appreciating and valuing the things that are closest to you.
3) Begin working on projects that are authentically you – projects that can develop the self, feed the soul, and become the foundation for getting yourself into states of flow.

Come to think of it, this might be a pretty good recipe for dealing with a lot of scenarios or emotions that you need to grow through. Flow, of course, is the nirvana of experience and high performance. It's just about time to reveal what flow is!

Part II

Rules of Engagement

1.   I will not Tweet.

2.   I will check email at two pre-designated times a day
(once in the morning, and once in the evening) and I will NOT
check email on the weekend. I will spend one hour maximum
online each time (recognizing that this is a very liberal guideline).

3.   I will only check Facebook during my pre-designated
email hours.

4.   I will enable Google Chat only during my pre-designated
email hours and can update my Google Chat status during this
time only.

5.   I will allow Google Latitude to update my location each
time I change states or countries, but I won't check to see where
I am *unless I'm actually lost or need a map*.

6.   No following blogs.

7.   No iGoogle.

8.   I will keep the Pavlovian, adrenaline/dopamine/endorphin
catalyzing, flashing green light on my Droid disabled.

9.   A few text messages a day is OK. (This includes direct
messages from Twitter).

10.   Checking LinkedIn about once a week is OK.

11.   Try to stay away from checking for new earthquakes.

Notes:

- The idea here is that my online time is carefully bounded.

- Either I'm *totally online*, or *totally not*.

- This does not solve the problem of "healthy use of mobile device," so we'll just ignore that for now.

- A major assumption is that the green blinking Droid light is disabled until further notice.

6/21/2010 (Monday)

It's the first day of summer, and the first day of my second cycle of improvement. Today, I get to adjust my Rules of Engagement with the online world based on the lessons learned in the first cycle, moving a little more in the direction I'd like to go (sustainably). Whereas the past cycle of improvement was focused on breaking old habits and excavating the mass of tangled emotions, ugliness, and conditioning, the new cycle (out of necessity) will focus on rebuilding and reconstructing.

> Headed to Führershauptquartiere for the day
> 8:15AM on 6/21/2010 from paper-journal

> At the GSO airport with my mother
> 8:51PM on 6/21/2010 from paper-journal

<u>Realization</u>: Funny how you don't even think about being online when you're too busy doing "real life" stuff for a day!

6/22/2010 (Tuesday)

"Atlanta passenger Human Bong, please report to Gate 29."
I kid you not. (in Memphis)
6:06AM on 6/22/2010 from paper-journal

The rarefied Rocky Mountain air is hazy today, and aloft with cottonwood dust and butterflies, so thick with summer that I don't even mind my burning eyes. I am at home. The gravity here over this spot on the Earth anchors the strings of my heart like no other. This is the distant horizon that so reliably soothes my shattered soul.

Pearl Street, then mtg at http://www.naropa.edu
12:54PM on 6/22/2010 from paper-journal

Editorial Comment: We are now on Mountain Time.

This is also the only place in the world I know of where you can grab a slice of Obama Stimulus Pizza, head a little farther down the street and catch your breath at the oxygen bar, get immersed in a loud *Om Mane Padme Hom* at the bookstore, and then catch an impromptu band of people who've never seen each other before as they cacophonally belt out a new tune. This is Boulder, if you haven't already guessed.

6/23/2010 (Wednesday)

Yesterday, I flowed all day, despite reconnecting to Google Chat and having some fine conversations. I reintroduced one of the key technologies that was driving me nuts, and was still able to fully and completely engage myself in the "real world." And how did I accomplish this? By asking two very easy questions: 1) What *else* could I be doing right now that's *not online*? And 2) What is the most authentic thing I could be doing with myself, and for myself, right now? Developing that uniquely authentic me? On the first question, I always had ideas, but (*sigh*) it would take *energy* to actually get out and *do them*. Solution to that? *Slicing.* Just take a step and do the slice of "getting in the car." Once in the car, with your keys in hand, you're *bound* to go *somewhere*. You are not likely to get out of the car, close the door, and return to the unmotivated spot you were in before.

> Benefit of jet lag: 6am swimming. It was awesome
> 10:34AM on 6/23/2010 from paper-journal

This morning, I woke up in a similar scenario. It was 5am, and I was wide awake. I spent time with my email for a while, wrote some long responses (immune from the email scorpion, since i'd gotten so much rest the night before), and then came to a crossroads. What is the most authentic thing I could be doing right now? The answer was crystal clear: swimming. Oh, but that takes so much energy. You have to get your bathing suit on, walk downstairs, head to the other side of the hotel... what a project. But ah, slicing! I sliced on my bathing suit, then decided that it was silly to be wearing my bathing suit in my room with nowhere to go, then sliced out the room door and down the elevator. Once I got to the pool area, there was no sense not going in, and the next thing you know I'd done 10 laps, was feeling invigorated, and headed back upstairs. Yeah!

Realization: The more I'm out there *living*, the less I'm tweeting – or even thinking about it. I *am* my *own life*!

6/24/2010 (Thursday)

Flow, flow, flow. When you are busy, and enjoying life, and enjoying friends, and pursuing new opportunities, there is no time for sadness or longing or feelings that are anything less than productive. There is only time for *using the moment you have*, right here and right now, to do the most authentic activity you can possibly slice.

> A pyramid & soon, Tsehay's excellent spicy mushrooms @ raskassas in Boulder
> 5:44PM on 6/24/2010 from paper-journal

If a distant horizon is soothing to a shattered soul, the absent air at 12,186 ft that complements a hundred mile visibility could pacify as many souls as the horizons you can't count. The drive on Trail Ridge Road was precipitous, thanks to the chasms and cracks in what was left of the road after the harshest of winters in a while. The snow was still packed six to ten feet high in places, with waterfalls dripping from beneath the glaciers to find their gradient paths downhill.

The sheer challenge of the cratered road quickly made me recover from the regret of passing up that Bloody Mary at Claire's in Estes Park. Even a sniff of vodka and I might have willingly plummeted off the alpine tundra meadows and into eternity. (Note: I would not even be thinking about this beverage had I not been initially introduced to it by @morphatic this past May 8. Had I imbibed, he could have unwillingly contributed to my mortality today.)

"There sure are a lot of rocks up here," my friend Vicky commented. She and I spend easy time together, just like we have for the past decade, ever since we did hard time as next door neighbors – just a jaunt south of here in Highlands Ranch. "Maybe that's why they call them the Rocky Mountains," I responded. I select from a portfolio of intelligent comments, and so does she; it's one of the traits of our friendship that keeps us forever mildly entertained.

The Bloody Mary from those coordinates on the Earth's surface will now be deferred to a later date. The gentle of the jazz, the thin blue breeze, and the stark rocky outcroppings fixed the scene in my mind's eye; liquid and landscape are eager to be consumed some other summer's afternoon.

Elk are always my favorite. They are solid, earthy, and give you blank looks when they lumber into traffic and nestle into giant elk-loaves on the toasty pavement, sunning their elk antlers haphazardly to underscore the idea that *this was their road* before it was even paved. They are pensive and executive. Atop Trail Ridge, a convention of grazers above the treeline (large and small, antlers and no-antlers, medium-sized trainees, and the tiny and freshly hatched) followed one another, forty to fifty strong across the highway. Some were a little more paranoid and anxiety-ridden than others. None had mobile devices, or even opposable thumbs.

It is very easy to *flow* when you are following the rules, and you have a *schedule* that is not so extreme that you violate Rule 1 by interjecting the Anxiety and Impatience productivity blocks. There are 8 rules.

"1. Clear goals: an objective is distinctly defined; immediate feedback; one knows instantly how well one is doing.

2. The opportunities for acting decisively are relatively high, and they are matched by one's perceived ability to act.

3. Action and awareness merge; one-pointedness of mind.

4. Concentration on the task at hand; irrelevant stimuli disappear from consciousness, worries and concerns are temporarily suspended.

5. A sense of potential control.

6. Loss of self-consciousness, transcendence of ego boundaries, a sense of growth and of being part of some greater entity.

7. Altered sense of time, which usually seems to pass faster.

8. Experience becomes autotelic: if several of the previous conditions are present, what one does becomes autotelic, or worth doing for its own sake."
     Csikszentmihalyi, *The Evolving Self*, p. 178-179

Why was it so easy to get into flow today? Easy: I followed all the rules. 1) Clear goals. Leave south Denver by 9am, drive around Estes Park and Rocky Mountain National Park, then return to Boulder in time for 4:45pm meeting at Naropa. 2) I could change my mind at any time and do something more authentic, if I so desired. 3) Focus on the road, the potholes, the elk: only one goal – go slow and don't fall off the cliff, thousands of feet to your demise. 4) See previous. 5) As long as the brakes don't fail, and that giant Arrow tourist bus doesn't sideswipe me into the ravine deep below, I'll be good. 6) I am a part of this beautiful corner of the Earth that is home. 7) How many hours have we been checking out elk and rocks? It never gets old. 8) I just love being here for what it is... and the opportunity to be a stone in this majestic landscape. I am one.

I love everyone at @raskassas in Boulder. Always sad to leave here
6:42PM on 6/24/2010 from paper-journal

6/25/2010 (Friday)

I have traveled many miles today. Left my hotel room at the Denver airport around 4:45am, took off at 7am, landed in San Diego at 8:15am Pacific Time, and drove a couple hundred miles up the coast to Santa Monica and back. Had a great dinner with Brett and Rebecca (my brother and sister in-laws) and their second-grader Colin at Houston's in Irvine. I spent much of my ride, before and after, contemplating the *perils of false authenticity*. We'll discuss it tomorrow.

> What's left of me is exhausted
> 9:42PM on 6/25/2010 from paper-journal

Editorial Comment: We are now on Pacific Time.

6/26/2010 (Saturday)

It's been nearly 36 hours since I left Colorado, and it's taken
about all that time to recover from the debilitating cottonwood allergy that left me tired and achy with burning eyes and
a scratchy throat. (I have a remarkable talent for planning trips
around the height of my personal allergic bliss.) I could have
taken some Benadryl, which works wonders for the symptoms,
but I didn't want to be sleepy because there was just too much
of the nourishing Colorado landscape and healing air to ingest.
I didn't sleep much while I was there, as if I didn't want to miss
out on even the tiniest minute. It's my place of power.

> Registration for SPIE starts in an hour. Astro techies are
> starting to trickle in.
> 3:20PM on 6/26/2010 from paper-journal

On my drive up the Pacific Coast Highway yesterday, I mentioned that my thoughts had turned towards the perils of false
authenticity. Ironically, it was the cottonwoods that raised the
subject with me, because my worst sniffly achiness didn't kick in
until a few hours before takeoff from Colorado, as if my adrenaline and emotions had pushed away the bulk of the symptoms *so
as not to interfere with me until I could no longer deny them.* I basically shut off my allergies until I had some time and mental space
to deal with them.

Now what the heck does this have to do with authenticity?
First of all, let me establish that this is a really liberal analogy,
so please be patient if the pieces don't connect for you. Here
goes. My body's natural, authentic response to cottonwood

dust floating through the air is to get sick. Itchy eyed, sniffly nosed sick. But being sick would have interrupted my Coloradan nirvana, and I had a lot of *fear* that my plans might be derailed. The fear was apparently so significant that it completely overwhelmed my body's authentic reaction to the floating cottonwood.

> Crying baby downstairs since 11am. Maybe he will run out of steam soon.
> 8:28PM on 6/26/2010 from paper-journal

Overcoming sickness, even temporarily, can be a positive manifestation of emotions overcoming your authentic reaction to something. Unfortunately, there are a lot of cases where the manifestations are negative or detrimental. Afraid of losing a job you dislike? Fear of being cut off can make you work harder, look happier, act spunkier – if only temporarily. Afraid of losing a relationship? Even if you're unhappy and you deeply desire to be released from the bonds, if you're confronted with that distinct possibility, fear can completely overwhelm your personality and authenticity – and you'll be happy and into it until your real self gets tired of pretending. Some people can pretend for an awfully long time, though. Not only are they asleep at the wheel in doing so, but they're truly missing out on life (in the same ways that I have been since I developed my nasty Twitter and Facebook habit).

I am weaning myself back on to a healthy, controlled interaction with my technology and social media. I have been checking my email about 3 times a day, and I allow myself to turn Google Chat on. It has been useful, and has not consumed me. I may try facebooking a little later this week.

A friend sent me a little snippet about codependency in relationships that made me start chewing on the notion that maybe I've got a codependent virtual soul. Here's a couple sentences from that article:

> "The next time I walked into a bookstore I was drawn to the Addiction/Self-Help section. I picked up three books that had been suggested by my friend and read them cover to cover. I started to really examine the idea that some people are so obsessed with another's life that they ignore their own feelings, thoughts, emotions and goals."
>
> Author unknown

Ever think about a codependent relationship with a *group* of virtual people who have all been conveniently prepackaged into one highly refined, corn syrup laden, calorie packed entity called your *social network*? I might have to Google a little more on that idea tomorrow. Or maybe not.

6/27/2010 (Sunday)

Who decides that Sunday morning would be a great time to start a professional conference?? I'd rather this SPIE thing start tomorrow… my most authentic activity right now, I think, would be sitting around drinking coffee and reading novels. But I'll do my duty, and slice my way out the door and over to the conference center.

> A day that is scheduled from 8am to 9pm goes quickly
> 9:09PM on 6/27/2010 from paper-journal

It is surprisingly pleasant to reconnect with people who have been sporadic portions of your life for a decade. That's what I did today at the conference, which is a gathering of engineers, astronomers and technology geeks who build giant telescopes. Big telescopes, like the Hubble; telescopes in space and telescopes on mountaintops. There is more intergalactic knowledge in this crowd than on the Enterprise. There are also more Japanese people, young and old (all with mobile devices), than one might find in any other part of the universe (except their own).

The most surprising part of this gathering, so far, is its mimicry of another place entirely. Even though I am in the middle of landlocked San Diego's Mission Valley, several miles inland, I'm trapped at a "resort" with no car. (That's not the curiosity.) The odd part is that I don't feel like I'm in San Diego at all — I keep thinking I'm in Hilo. This little microcosm of the eastern slope has been directly imported from the 1960's, architecture and attitude, and the pseudo-Banyans are complemented by the ever so slight aroma of maybe-mold. I am not alone. Twice I have mentioned this similitude in conversation, and twice I have prompted reputable engineers and scientists with appropriate experiential knowledge to choke on their coffee, equally entertained as I that we're trapped in this Hilo-like niche of southern California. (Because once you pull out of this "resort" complex, off its 20 acres, you return to San Diego proper and escape from all consequences of potential microcosmic tsunamis. And I am using my quotation marks in exactly the tongue-in-cheek way they are intended.)

Realization: Sitting through dull academic and engineering talks compels one to check the Droid frequently and furiously for emails. (Twitter is still off limits.)

6/28/2010 (Monday)

I had forgotten to mention it yesterday, but I spent five minutes on Facebook between yesterday and today. The demonic possession has been unhinged. I even Did Something Important by sharing a link posted by my friend Matt Welsh, advertising *The Social Network Movie* or some such, where he plays the role of *Harvard Professor*. Actually, he isn't *in* the movie, it's someone else playing him – he just *is* the *Harvard Professor*. Which, in my opinion, is even cooler.

> Day 4 of 7 in San Diego
> 8:58AM on 6/28/2010 from paper-journal

I have been in an uncommon meditative state these past few days since arriving in my little Hilo bubble. Time is simultaneously moving furiously while it hangs in the balance of then and now, tentative and silent. The part of me that is not Doing Nothing has been eating pretzels. The pretzels, too, are furious and silent, reminding me I must pick up a coffee and arrive at my conference session in precisely 59 minutes, or else. My shoes have also gotten bigger.

> "Scientists have examined butterfly trees and found them chemically and physically identical to the trees around them. Yet no other tree will do. Investigators have camouflaged a tree's color, altered its scent. The monarchs were not fooled. Another of nature's mysterious constants. A butterfly always knows when it is *there*."
>
> Tom Robbins, *Another Roadside Attraction*, p. 49

I am still looking for my tree.

Fish tacos. Elixir of life, at least this week
8:36PM on 6/28/2010 from paper-journal

6/29/2010 (Tuesday)

I have discovered that there are two great productivity blocks, unique ones, that interfere with one's ability to commit thoughts to paper. The first is *not having a pen that embraces the motions of your hand.* Without a faucet as a writing utensil, the words just fall out one at a time and bounce like mercury down the drain. The second is *piling things you don't want to forget in your hotel room* on top of your writing notebook. Room key(s), lighter, *do not disturb* sign, memory stick(s), eyeglasses, Droid, drugs, deodorant. The essentials, though forever found, sometimes crowd out creativity like too many leftovers in the refrigerator.

Oh, and there is a third (please revise my earlier estimate); lack of desperation. Words splat onto the page like wild springtime tears when the soul strains to hear its own migratory call. Or when there is a deadline. But there is more to life than water and dried pretzels, and just because technology isn't stretching my arms off today doesn't mean it won't try to do it tomorrow. It's a lonely see-saw, with only the pretzels sitting on the other side of the plank.

> Time for more elixir of life
> 11:58AM on 6/29/2010 from paper-journal

> fmd: fun moderated discussions and a sweater, bc it's 60 deg F
> 6:16PM on 6/29/2010 from paper-journal

Sometimes, you just want to run away. Most times you can't, for example, when the offender is the foot itself. When there is no way out, sometimes there's no way *in*, either.

6/30/2010 (Wednesday)

Who am I? What am I supposed to be doing in life? These are all the ancient questions that bubble, boilingly, up to the surface when the wireless internet is out. And why, oh why, am I still immersed in this sixty degree wintry entrapment of almost-July San Diego (or is it just Hilo, slightly sniffling and under the weather?) Clearly, I am being thrust by the universe into that dungeon of forced deep thought, where there is *something* (*must be something*) to be uncovered, fueled by the delicate anguish of gazing at the chlorine blue and floating noodle reds, wielded by those who can swim in the winter (they're probably from Minnesota). It is a longing glance, impaled by the possibility that maybe I could jump in too – the kind of longing you might have for that blissful state of conquering death at the end of a torturous and much anticipated dentist's visit. (Bet you can't guess what's coming up for me in exactly two weeks).

There is no internet connection right now. I am twitching with discomfort. May the fleas of the virtual world find higher bandwidth pastures.

In the chill of the barefoot morning concrete, the whisper of barely fluxing electrons, the words appeared staccato and discrete on the blue powerpoint screen. *I am in love with an illusion*, maybe many of them, punctuated by the still of the Wi-Fi. To be in flow, I must build something, and right now I'm just *going through the motions*. And therein lies the problem. How can you build something you don't see, or more importantly, *struggle to feel?*

> Ran lightning talks at SPIE last night. The electrical engineers
> were particularly moved
> 8:18AM on 6/30/2010 from paper-journal

I think the difference between getting into flow and just going
through the motions all boils down to autotelic point 8: in flow,
the activity becomes *worth doing for its own sake*. The key word
here is worth. That's a value judgment, and not only an analytical
judgment, but a decision you *feel*. If you don't viscerally *feel* the
worth of an activity or a decision, it's going to be hard to slip
into that seductive one-pointedness of mind that stimulates the
freedom of flow.

BTW, I think I have discovered the poisonous arrow of
Facebook. It is the "Most Recent" tab that tremors with the
excitement and the trivia of the latest second's status updates.
The remainder of the site is far less Bacchanalian, and as a result,
more tolerant regarding integration into real life.

Realization: Avoid the "Most Recent" tab on Facebook to preserve sanity.

> Time to give my last talk… then I can drink and go home
> (tomorrow)
> 11:46AM on 6/30/2010 from paper-journal

The clouds have been hovering overhead (suppressing convec-
tion and light spirits) for days now – so long that I'd forgotten there was a blue sky still somewhere above it. The sun is
now out, and the solar astronomers are looking at it, directly
of course, with large pieces of very smart metal and mirrors
twisted illustriously into the shapes of telescopes. Ordinary
people staring directly into the sun might be shunned. These
guys… it's their job. They seem happy to see the sun as well,
perhaps rejoicing in the reappearance of their own personal
job security.

I think my long-term Twitter strategy will be "write-only"
6:41PM on 6/30/2010 from paper-journal

Capricorn, Aquarius, Pisces & Jones, I need my Neptune back
8:20PM on 6/30/2010 from paper-journal

It's the last night of the conference in San Diego, and I'm sitting in my lonely meditative room. I have a transparent plastic cup in front of me, lid firmly (I hope) attached, clear plastic straw jutting diagonally from the top, half empty with Karl Strauss Amber. It's almost classical. However, there is no way to adequately capture the blissful solitude of the moment in 140 characters or less. "I'm drinking beer through a straw" sounds rather commonplace, and much too straightforward for the sheer simplistic *magnitude* of it. "Packing and enjoying a beer in my room" makes me sound like the lush I'm not. It also has a tone that is reminiscent of tobacco and pipes. Plus, that tweet would confess that I'm alone, and I don't want to sound lonely or desperate. (I am slightly lonely, but desperately not desperate.) I *am*, however, self-censoring in a triumphant manner.

Who says you can't drink beer from a straw?
9:18PM on 6/30/2010 from paper-journal

Exeunt June. I have known you well.

"Darkened rolling figures move through prisms of no color
Hand in hand, they walk the night
But never know each other
Passioned pastel neon lights light up the jeweled traveler
Who, lost in scenes of smoke filled dreams
Finds questions, but no answers.

Startled eyes that sometimes see phantasmagoric
splendor
Pirouette down palsied paths
With pennies for the vendor
Salvation's yours for just the time it takes to pay the
dancer.
And once again such anxious men
Find questions, but no answers.

The night has gone and taken its infractions
While saddened eyes hope there will be a next one.

Sahara signs look down upon a world that glitters glibly
And mountain sides put arms around
The unsuspecting city
Second hands that minds have slowed are moving even
faster
Toward bringing down someone who's found
The questions, but no answers."

Michael Nesmith, Daily Nightly

7/1/2010 (Thursday)

Today is the last day of the SPIE astronomical instrumentation
conference, and after a quick dinner with one of the planning
committees tonight, I'll be headed to the airport and home.
There have been two great accomplishments this week: 1) over
80% of the time, *I* was in control of my technology and my life
(and my technology was not in control of me), and 2) I definitely
tapped into an autotelic experience while being here at the conference. As one of the Conference Chairs, I can definitely exercise a measure of control; I am part of something *much* greater
and bigger than myself and it feels good, helping to connect
over two thousand scientists and engineers with one another in
creative and unique ways. As a result, it is certainly (in my own
judgment of value) worth doing for its own sake. Another thing
worth doing for its own sake is making the little 0.3mi hike to
the Starbucks stand to get my last early morning San Diego latte
for a while.

> Setting off on my early AM hike to Starbucks
> 7:36AM on 7/1/2010 from paper-journal

Ah, latte. So a couple of weeks ago, I was musing on the phrase
"that's how I roll." The contemplation hasn't ceased, even
through the phrase has cropped up noticeably less than the
hundred or so times it did in the beginning. Instead of the little
voice in my head chewing on it, though, it's actually been the
little voice *behind* the little voice doing all the work lately – although granted, it's hard to tell whether it was really that voice,
or the one behind *it*, or the one behind *IT*, ad infinitum (as I gaze

through the slightly curved pathway descending deep into the mirror).

I had thought that the "that's how I roll" phrase referred to someone who routinely gets into flow. Now I'm not so sure. I've heard several people make this remark who clearly aren't "flow-ers." I think they must just be going through the motions, fragrant or not. So if you can *roll* by either flowing or just going through the motions, what's the common thread? Both approaches have their benefits – for example (for me), going to the dentist is most assuredly an exercise of going through the motions, because I do not consider such an event to be worth doing for the sake of doing. No way. Flow requires attachment to a situation, but detachment from ego concerns. Going through the motions requires detachment from a situation, yet in this state, ego concerns are irrelevant and can even play the starring role without incident. *Roll*, on the other hand, seems to imply a sort of detached agility where you don't let your ego get in the way, you consciously aim to detach from all the veils that could confuse you, and you move in concert with all changes – planned and unplanned – with compassion, constructiveness, dignity, and grace. (That sounds nice, doesn't it.)

> Day 7 of 7 in San Diego
> 8:50AM on 7/1/2010 from paper-journal

I've been feeling lately that I just can't shake this subtle discontent. Even though I've been detoxed for a month now, I still feel trapped. The intrusive thoughts that compelled me to check that blinking green Droid light hundreds of times a day are now thinking me into the dusty oblivion of checking email every 8 to 10 minutes. Have I learned nothing?

The train may have communicated an ancient secret to me this afternoon, though. We took off from the conference compound (that is, me, a guy named John Ford from West Virginia, and @

rduplain and his Twitterless wife Tekla – oh my, that almost sounds like a disparaging statement – sorry, guys) for a Mexican lunch in Old Town. It's a 2-stop glide down the Trolley train line if you're on the Green line and if you were where we were standing. The ride comes every 10 minutes, and of course, as soon as we got there – no train and lots of waiting riders. Good, I thought... the train's bound to arrive any second. Spectators and potential riders crowded around, starting to discuss between themselves the tardiness of the transportation. 10 minutes more, 15 minutes, 20 minutes. The questions brought no train. Three trains, then, going the other direction (there is no conservation of trains, I presume?) But no trains for us. Useless. I wasn't the only restless soul; the buzz was palpable.

"Do you think we should just go to lunch somewhere else?" I asked @rduplain. No train. No promise of a train. "Maybe the train won't come. Maybe it's stuck, or not running today. Maybe it's out of service." I was very good at making lots of excuses on the train's behalf.

He gave me a little smirk as the train pulled up behind me in mid-complaint. Ancient lesson? *The train never shows up until after you've given up waiting for it.*

My reflections are slowing down. Either I'm figuring something out, or I'm slowly realizing that I'm not figuring anything out. I just mentioned to Ron that I wrote a full 140 pages during the first 21 days of my disconnected project. "140 pages?" he asked. "That's kind of poetic... a self-similarity with Twitter." Maybe there are deeper forces at work, perhaps the positrons are adding some enthusiastic glee to the mix, subconsciously architecting my moves with mischief. Or maybe not. (You're giving up 140 characters, they ask? Watch this, I'll compel you to write 140 pages instead.)

> Enjoying the San Diego sun and 75 deg w/ @rduplain and Tekla at SPIE

2:55PM on 7/1/2010 from paper-journal

I have only seen 2 ppl here in this 2500+ crowd who I can't
ID as male or female
3:24PM on 7/1/2010 from paper-journal

It's been a random afternoon. The sun is setting (OK, I guess
that's not exactly random), the talks are over, the drink tickets are being joyously exchanged for libations, and the Middle
Eastern tunes broadcast from the squeaky wheel on the A/V
cart are being breathed in cacophonous cadences as the vehicle
trips over each crooked brick.

There are many non sequitur thoughts that intrude and recol-
lect into your consciousness in the middle of a dull talk. For example, when I was in elementary school, I always thought that a
sous-chef was the guy who prepared the *sous-shi*.

7/2/2010 (Friday)

I flew overnight from San Diego to Charlotte, then over to Charlottesville (where I live), was picked up at the airport by Todd and our five-year-old Alex, and immediately headed north on 29, west on 33, up on I-81 and over on I-84 to the in-laws' abode in Connecticut. Whirlwinds leave no room for tweeting, and barely space for any thinking that surpasses fitful sleep or vacuous ground-gazing.

> SPIE is over… now back to real life (sort of). See you in Amsterdam in 2012 :)
> 10:15PM on 7/2/2010 from paper-journal

Editorial Comment: We are now on Eastern Time.

I've been taking long walks since the start of technology detox a month ago, and apparently it's working. When I walked into my in-laws' house, my father-in-law's greeting was classic: "You look slimmer. What happened, they run out of food in Colorado and California?" :)

7/3/2010 (Saturday)

There is no greater feeling of renewal than taking a shower after you haven't had one in far too many days, and you're really
dirty. I had the distinct pleasure this morning of sloughing off
2,800 miles of artificial airplane air conditioning, grub from my
unconscious head zonked on the food trays, grime picked up
from my shoeless toes stepping through the full body scanner
and onto the questionable carpet beyond, shoes then worn well
too long, the sweat of passing out in the sunny passenger's side
post-pickup, the edgy chlorine of gas station bathrooms, and of
course the general staleness of slow-oozed jet lag. Now, on to
bigger and dirtier things.

The only better shower I've had in my life was on March 26,
1992 (some people remember birthdays and anniversaries; I
remember when cleanliness elevates you to near-godliness). We
had just returned from spelunking – crawling around for hours
in the silty pit of an underground playground – a starry group of
experiential high school geology students who had just shared
community with the bats, a dirty five hour van ride in uniformly
soaking jeans, and (at least for me) blond braids that had taken
on the hue of the cappuccino colored subterranean. I'd ceremoniously dipped those pigtails in the mush every time a stalactite
embraced one side of me, or that time when a crawl through a
foot-high tunnel got a bit too intimate. We were all silt-logged to
the bone, the moisture's waffle pattern on every finger and toe
in attendance. Upon arriving back at school, where we all lived,
we had to hit the showers immediately to prevent leaving cave
mud in places we (or the successors who would next occupy
our rooms) would find it weeks or years later. There were three

shower stalls on the Reynolds Second C hall – one for Carolyn, one for Ryn, and the third for me. There was no shortage of editorial pleasure as we swapped shampoos and commented on how awakening it was to see the tone of our respective skins emerge from the muck.

Headed to Gelston Castle in NY to see Furthur
11:09AM on 7/3/2010 from paper-journal

(The rest of the day consisted of driving 190mi, hanging out in a two mile long traffic jam with other beer-drinking detainees, hiking through Shakedown Street, and checking my Droid to see whether I was moving slower or faster than time itself. :)

7/4/2010 (Sunday)

It's a holiday! If you can't stay off the computer for one day, especially one where everyone's supposed to be celebrating *something*, then something is wrong.

> Heading up to Hitchcock Lake in CT w/Alex for some decentralized fireworks
> 7:53PM on 7/4/2010 from paper-journal

7/5/2010 (Monday)

In *Care of the Soul*, Thomas Moore explains through archetypes and myth that part of the journey anyone goes through is to encounter and work through their own unique collection of emotions. Some will be enjoyable, some will be ecstatic and hopeful, some will be challenging and uncomfortable, others will be confusing and nebulous, and the most transformational will be so difficult that you are reluctant to let them transform you. Without any of these feelings and emotions, he notes, the soul would not be satisfied – because the soul needs good and bad, intense and shallow, and even lime green as well as chartreuse, in order to be fully nurtured. The tough hours and days make the beautiful ones all that more enjoyable. The first warm toasty spring day is always more satisfying after months of a bitter winter.

> Not all who wander are lost
> 8:33PM on 7/5/2010 from paper-journal

No Wi-Fi and no direction today. I feel lost and not in control, completely detached from the light and promise of flow. I'm even one step behind "sitting online waiting for something to happen."

Moore talked about one person he was counseling who came in and announced "I'm deeee-pressed." He misheard her and thought she said "I need deep rest." He realized that maybe this slip of the ear uncovered a truth: sometimes, to heal the soul, you just need *deep rest* every now and then. Don't feel bad about it, don't question it, don't try to push harder and get to solutions you think you need faster. Just rest. The solutions will eventually emerge when you are ready for them, when they are ready for you, and no quicker and no earlier. It's like that train that you wait for, and wait for, and wait even more for – and it won't arrive until you relinquish the act of waiting itself.

In the meantime, *deep rest*. And possibly thumbing through the National Enquirer.

7/6/2010 (Tuesday)

I spent a few hours online this morning finishing up an application review for the Baldrige National Quality Program. I checked Facebook once, and was on Google Chat briefly, but did not feel the pangs of social media envy whatsoever. Progress is being made. But now that I'm offline again today, I'm realizing that my imbalance in the virtual world may just be a reflection of an imbalance in the real world. Here's why: 1) I'm sitting around waiting for something to happen, and without a computer in front of me, I'm doing it entirely without continuously hitting the "Refresh" button. 2) I am having a difficult time distinguishing between *boredom* and *relaxation*.

> We're supposed to go swimming in the lake once everyone gets their act together. Good luck
> 1:26PM on 7/6/2010 from paper-journal

I think the difference is illuminated by the concept of flow. Being in flow, whether it's traditionally "relaxing" or conversely challenging, will typically yield a sense of renewal and contentment. Additionally, and by definition, flow is *not* boredom. Relaxation, on the other hand, can completely embody the potential for boredom; that would be relaxation *without purpose*. Any deeply relaxing activity I can think of, other than sleeping (which can itself be fitful) enables a person to get into flow. Swimming, sailing in the breeze, kayaking through the nooks and crannies of the lakeshore – all flow inducing, even without the water element. Sitting here waiting for other people to make up their minds for two and a half hours about when we should actually head to the lake to try and get into flow – well, that produces no flow at all, just frustration and waiting and a total feeling of having no control over my day.

> "In her face I notice a terrible beauty. Like the terrible beauty of nature itself. It reveals to me two facts. One: she loves me deeply. Two: she is completely indifferent as to whether she ever sees me again."
> Tom Robbins, *Another Roadside Attraction*, p. 336

In the midst of boredom, relaxation, flow, and detoxification from technology, the fundamental fabric of my relationship with technology (and possibly everyone else) has shifted. I'm the only one left standing.

7/7/2010 (Wednesday)

The pioneers indulged their itchy feet and hitched up their wagons to explore the rivers and streams and rocks of the western horizons. I simply turned the Tahoe onto the New York Thruway, I-90, and followed the sun all day. Todd and I spent some time at the Holiday Inn bar in Rochester after driving all day. Note that I didn't say "spent time together" – he was glued to his Blackberry. I am noticing this behavior in other people much, much more these days. I got a healthy dose of my sad old medicine.

Today: Rochester. Tomorrow: Buffalo/Lewiston ArtPark
9:20PM on 7/7/2010 from paper-journal

7/8/2010 (Thursday)

[This day intentionally left blank.]

7/9/2010 (Friday)

We woke up in Lewiston, New York, spitting distance from
Ontario (which was visible; we could have potentially spit to
it right from our hotel room patio). We spent the night before
at another concert at the ArtPark, a tiny little venue on the
Niagara River where you can see the water rushing from Lake
Erie in the south to Lake Ontario in the north. We created a
cataclysmic thunderstorm of reconnecting with real life shortly
thereafter; there were only a few idealistic tornadoes, but the
landscape was swept clean in preparation for rebuilding.

As is usually the case, we found fun and quirky people to spend
the show with – this time, Justin and Janelle, the yoga instructors
from Michigan. It was nearly 100 degrees, so I had to coat myself
with icicles from the beer cooler all day just to remain cogent.
Janelle, a first generation Chaldean girl (who in fact just might *be*
the seventh veil), gave me one of her mom's excellent Chaldean
cheese rolls. Justin likes Pacifico beer. These are the non se-
quiturs that you carry in your memory forever after random
chance encounters. However, Janelle and I are now Facebook
friends, so there may very well be non-random non-chance encounters in the future. (But I won't recount the entire day, for
fear of sounding like Hunter S. Thompson, because *my* Gonzo
reporting is *all real*.)

> Ended up in Bennington, VT. Where's Waldo?
> 8:19PM on 7/9/2010 from paper-journal

I'm back up to 39 messages sitting dormant in my Inbox. This
"Inbox Zero" thing requires not only continuous dedication,

but also (I'm finding out) – the ability to completely ignore the looming disaster that may snowball in your email if you stop actively managing it. *Detachment* is the philosophical key.

And I'm almost dried out from the spontaneous three-dot downpour at Niagara Falls yesterday. Todd and I typically visit places like this in only the most poetic and inopportune weather. Yesterday was no exception.

7/10/2010 (Saturday)

In the beginning, I posed the question that's been in the back of my mind for the past six weeks: If I disconnect from my virtual life, will I reconnect with my *real* one? There are two answers to this query. 1) Yes. 2) But what you uncover, what you find in your *real life* (once you slip off that avatar costume) might not be entirely pleasant and you might not want to deal with it. However, in the offline state of being, you will have plenty of time for these other problems to compete for your attention, and ultimately (and uncomfortably) win.

> South St. Café in Bennington, VT makes a fine latte
> 10:57AM on 7/10/2010 from paper-journal

Have I mentioned that when you finally stop waiting for the train, it arrives? That's been a theme in my life the past few days. It makes me realize that I should *relax my expectations* concerning what I'm going to learn, or what I should learn, as a result of the process of disconnecting. I've been waiting at the platform for Insight to arrive, staring down the long bend of the tracks, wondering if the train's even running at all.

But if you could read the invisible ink between the letters and the lines, the train would be there already; you would be in the midst of an epic tale of transformation. And in addition to that, there would be bloody battles, and large acquisitions of arable farmland, followed by quiet and unnerving defeats, and long winters without food, and carefully executed arson, and loves gained and loves lost (sometimes simultaneously, sometimes serially), and sometimes just being lost, or swimming. There would be no

need to stretch for the prose to describe the insight, because
the picture would be cast from that place beyond illusion and
linguistics. But perhaps you are one of the lucky ones whose
eyes are attuned to the imperceptible stories, and to you I say,
let's go there; let's live out our story.

And have I ever mentioned how much I love thunderstorms?
The rhythmic click of the hail on the window, the passive acceptance of the watery rumble, the journey to find riches in one's
own inner nature in total acceptance of outer loneliness? *The
louder and more violent, the more luxuriously cathartic.*

> It's not about whether you survive the storm, but how well
> you can dance in the rain —sign on VT rd
> 11:52AM on 7/10/2010 from paper-journal

Long car rides are perfect for stressful, tentative, exploratory,
probing conversations. In the natural flow of the asphalt road,
there is less of a burden to actually *solve* a problem, and more of
an evolutionary push to assimilate it and get in tune with all five
(or more) senses of it, just *being* it, while letting it exist a little
off to the side of you. I keep reminding myself that nothing has
ever turned out wrong even when the cataclysms of life have
been emotionally murderous. I look back and see an elegant
order in all things, peppered with a scintillating sense of how
everyone, everywhere, is connected and entangled imperviously.
There is an orchestra striking notes at a frequency that not even
dogs and teenagers are aware of, but it's there, linking all of our
thoughts and actions together to create synchronicities beyond
our wildest dreams.

But to get there takes time, patience, and a ride that will be
no shorter and no longer than it ultimately needs to be. To get
through, you have to *roll with it* — not getting into flow, not going
through the motions, but allowing *time itself* to work through

184

you and with you and in you, while you respond to change with dignity, grace, and hopeful anticipation.

I don't enjoy airplane rides at all — in fact, more often than not, this is the one activity in life that consistently and reliably stirs a panic attack in me, so I spend my most of my rides doped up (with sincere thanks to my primary care physician). So while I'm sitting in my airplane seat, that little voice inside my head turns into both diplomat and counselor to my subconscious. "What would you rather," it asks, "to end the airplane trip *now*, in mid-journey, or to spend the time that's needed to get to your destination and *then* arrive?" Clearly, the negative consequences of the first option are both substantial and dire, so I usually respond by admitting that yes, I'd rather invest anxious and un-settled time in the ride and ultimately get to where I need to go safely, and in one piece.

There is no difference between the anxiety of a plane ride and the unknowing that comes with difficult situations and major transitions in life. Sometimes you just need to *roll with it*, let time do its job to propel you to your destination, and let entangle-ment work its strange and incomprehensible magic. The world has been around a lot longer than you or I have. It will take your hand and guide you, if only you sweep all those idiotic and trivial distractions from interfering with your ability to hear the move-ment of those ancient voices, especially the announcement that the hand is outstretched.

Realization: Something good is coming my way!

> Shall we go, you and I while we can, through the transitive nightfall of diamonds?
> 10:31PM on 7/10/2010 from paper-journal

There's a solar eclipse and a new moon (by definition) tomor-row. A time of endings and new, surprising beginnings. A time to reflect on lessons learned and all of the positive, amazing things to bring forward into your life in the future. A time to work the magic of the 42ⁿᵈ day.

Douglas Adams claims that his choice of the number 42 as the answer to the ultimate question of life, the universe and everything was random – a joke with no well thought-out meaning or punch line. Well, Mr. Adams, I think you may have accidentally stumbled upon a Möbius chord of personal development and continuous improvement. Yes, you *can* really break a habit or define a new behavior pattern in 21 days. And guess what happens if you keep reflecting on the meaning of life and how you've shifted it for yourself over the *next* 21 days? You get your own personal answer to the ultimate question – *at least for just right now* – and that's *the only moment that counts.* Ever.

(And in the meantime, don't panic.)

7/11/2010 (Sunday)

NEW MOON

SOLAR ECLIPSE

DAY 42 (unless I can't count, which is entirely possible)

Things begin, and things end. Even the process of disintegration reaches a stage where there is no remaining potential for decay or breakdown, a place where the natural order seeks to once again build, and create, and flourish. The process of renewal ends when that which has been plundered or razed (or just plain old wiped out) is repopulated with the spirit and vigor of abundance. Sometimes, people or places or situations or ideas have simply outlived their useful time, and it becomes apparent that one of the entities in the mix (either us or them) must move on. Sometimes, it's a little more complicated – when the veils fall, and illusions drop off into dust, the meaning we assign to those elements of life can drastically metamorphose in the blink of an eye.

This does not mean that I have all the answers. In fact, I may have none.

I love how – when you clear up the clutter and confusion in your own soul – synchronicities begin to abound, suggesting that you're on the right path. Uncommon words and curious phrases crop up with statistical significance. People with meaningful names randomly introduce themselves to you in crowds of ten thousands, as if the universe is nodding in agreement, tipping its hat to your newfound clarity and awareness. Friends and acquaintances turn you on to books and articles and inspirational phrases that deliver just the right message at the right moment, blissfully distanced from the messenger. Sometimes, relevant stuff just appears in the morning newspaper (but of course, if you're glued to the desktop or get your news exclusively through Yahoo or Twitter, you'd miss it):

> "[A relatively new Facebook user] found that a lot of friends were saying and doing *random things that kept intruding on her life.*
>
> In other words, Facebook is, as I said in the previous column, a time-sucker. In technical terms, the signal-to-noise ratio is very low.
>
> The experience of having a lot of friends on Facebook is much like that of the Mel Gibson character in 'What Women Want' – when he suddenly develops the ability to read minds, he's overwhelmed by a lot of random thoughts and has to focus on the ones that are most important."
>
> - Howard Fielding, "Facebook is a great way to keep in touch… sometimes," *Sunday Republican (Waterbury, CT)* on 7/11/2010

Overwhelmed by randomness. That's the curse of the interrupt-driven existence. It erodes the single-pointedness of mind and the sense of control that are so elemental in achieving flow, and sets you into a pattern where you're *content* sitting around waiting for something to happen – after all, so much is happening out there somewhere, there's just bound to be a gem, a glittering nugget of adrenaline for your next fix! The number one lesson from my technology detox project is along this thread:

Lesson 1: Don't sit around waiting for something to happen. Go *make* something happen instead! By taking steps to *make* something happen, you wrestle control from the interrupt-driven existence and open up your potential for getting into that flow state of optimal experience. (As a corollary to this, note that you should also have somewhat of a *schedule* for making things happen. Not too slack, not too aggressive, just something that will get you out of your house or otherwise out of your comfort zone where all those productivity killers camp out. I was *much* happier on the days I was obligated to do something with people, or to be somewhere at a set time.)

Things begin, and things end. And in suffering the slings and arrows of the death of an obsession (or maybe two), what emerges is a *wildly liberating soulfulness*. I do not want or need you, technology; you merely slip in and out of my life as appropriate, and under my direction, easily, without resistance or unwelcome randomness. You are a part of my life, but I do not live *in* or *through* you. The adrenaline and dopamine and angst have yielded to peace and detachment. This is how we can all just *roll with it* with dignity and grace, not knowing what comes next, and not *needing* to know every 140 characters of what's going on at the moment. (*This* is authenticity.)

I have buried old habits and birthed new ones. Twitter will survive for me, but in a write-only mode. Sorry, Twitter friends, you all may be perfectly competent in that world but it's too much for me to handle (for the most part). Facebook will remain dormant except for occasional visits and posts, kind of like dropping by the DMV. Google Chat will retain its esteemed status in my social portfolio, a safe haven where the personal connections are stronger, more meaningful, and more sparse. And I will probably never text again while driving, simply because in my newfound detachment, I realize that nothing is permanent – *especially urgency*. Everything can wait.

189

Lesson 2: Detachment is key. Keep your insatiable tape in the junk drawer. Train yourself: entertain a Digital Sabbath or a self-imposed limit on how many times a day (or hours a day) you'll allow yourself to check email or be online. Most importantly, detach from that false sense of smug accomplishment you might feel as "someone who can handle it" – someone who's mastered the multitasking of the interrupt-driven life. You may be able to handle the habit or the pattern, but can you handle what you're *missing out on?* (Oh, nevermind – those afflicted by digital blindness won't be able to see or feel the potential of that other world regardless.)

The pursuit of authenticity, once initiated, has no end. If it ends, that indicates that you were never on the path to authenticity in the first place, and you'll have to try starting it up again. Granted, the collective influence of ego and genes and culture is not only strong but undeniable; you can be shaken off the path just as passionately as you blazed the trail to get on it. But in addition to just being yourself, what does it really mean to pursue authenticity? Have I become closer to achieving this transcendental state by getting offline? The answer is yes, and James Park has the question.

> "Cast into the blind, purposeless whirl of existence, we must either choose our own lives or have our lives chosen for us by the social forces already in operation when we were born. There are no given, automatic meanings in human lives. We human beings must create whatever goals we will pursue...
>
> We *are* what we *pursue*. If we want to become more Authentic, we will devise our own reasons for living, which might go beyond what anyone has ever tried before...
>
> If you were completely free, how would you use your life?"
> - James Park, *Becoming More Authentic*
> http://www.tc.umn.edu/~parkx032/CY-AU.html

Another way of asking this is as follows: "Who would I be if I didn't know me?" Probably not the self-censored Tweeter, and maybe not even most of who you've decided to be so far. But have you shut out the buzz and examined your habits to see if you've ever *stopped to think about it* before?

One of the biggest questions that's plagued me over the past several weeks is: Who am I? What am I supposed to be doing with my life? Now the answer resonates: *to relentlessly pursue living authentically.* OK, so that sounds nice, but how can I make this actionable in my day to day life? I have some ideas, although several are not yet fully formed. One thing I can do is to be conscious of whatever activity is the most authentic for me at any given time, and go with it. A *clue* will be how effectively I can slip into the flow state of optimal experience; if I'm struggling to get there, I may wish to reconsider whether what I'm doing is a truly authentic reflection of who I am.

Realization: Many of the things that I've been doing that I *thought* were authentic reflections of who I am will be fading out over the next several months. I'd rather do nothing than not live authentically! I'd rather live a life that dances into and out of the flow state, being ultimately productive on a daily basis, than live one with no potential for liberation into a high quality of life – even if it means thoroughly transforming structures and relationships to achieve it. Calling this a "primal urge" would not even give the force justice.

Lesson 3: It doesn't matter who I am, how I've defined myself, or whether I can identify that elusive "purpose" that tells me what I should or should not be doing in life. What *matters* is that I am a *seeker*, committed to contribute to the world in a way that is constructive and that *authentically* resonates with my being. (The rest of the details will work themselves out, if only I *let go!*)

191

Being authentic, and living authentically, puts me in a position where I'm best able to get into flow and tap into the abundance of the universe. And although I'm not going to dedicate myself to the pursuit of happiness (after all, Thomas Moore emphatically suggests that the soul *needs* not only the light emotions but also the shadow, or else there would be no contrast or depth) – I will dedicate myself to the pursuit of authenticity. It's bound to contribute to a sense of satisfaction:

> "People who lead a satisfying life, who are in tune with their past and with their future – in short, people whom we would call 'happy' – are generally individuals who have lived their lives according to rules they themselves created... their goals are not selfish in any of the three senses of serving the genes, the culture, or the ego. They do what they do because they enjoy meeting the challenges of life, because they enjoy life itself. They feel that they are part of the universal order, and identify themselves with harmonious growth. It is this kind of self that will make survival into the third millennium possible."
>
> Csikszentmihalyi, *The Evolving Self*, p. 82

The feelings that lead to this cultivation of satisfaction are pure, simple and uncluttered. And the act of achieving flow through authenticity has amazing side effects, which I'll cover in lessons 4 and 5. In the meantime, you may wonder why I've so narcotically been focused on this flow state all these weeks. Even if I've mentioned it already, it's worth repeating:

> "Such feelings – which include concentration, absorption, deep involvement, joy, a sense of accomplishment – are what people describe as the best moments of their lives. They can occur almost anywhere, at any time, provided one is using psychic energy in a harmonious pattern. It is typically present when one is singing or

dancing, engaged in religious ritual or sports, when one is engrossed in reading a good book or watching a great performance. It is what the lover feels like talking to her beloved, the sculptor chiseling marble, the scientist engrossed in her experiment."

Csikszentmihalyi, *The Evolving Self*, p. 82

The flow state is the elixir of life! (Especially if you're not convinced that fish tacos are where it's at. Or if you don't like fish.) People get to the flow state in many different ways, but the end result, the invigorating and rejuvenating effect on the self and the inner life, is undeniable. Lesson 4 revolves around what you need to do to get closer to flow; lesson 5 is the fantastically amazing side effect.

Lesson 4: To get to the flow state, you first have to clear yourself of all the barriers and burdens that also inhibit and confuse authenticity. This means: 1) battling the productivity blocks of anxiety, ego, boredom, and impatience, 2) aggressively poking at and lifting the veils of ego, culture and genes – veils that convince us we *should* do something or *ought* to do something or *are obligated* to do something (even when we really don't want to, deep down!) and 3) when all else fails, taking little slices of life just to get moving, so you can capture the energy of 1) and 2).

Things begin, and things end. When you clear out all that unnecessary random clutter flowing into you through your virtual world, you open yourself to sweep out the real world clutter, resurface the potholes in your psyche, and get all that good energy flowing in a productive way. Now, there's a very curious lesson here that only some of you might find meaningful, and I'm only newly starting to see it emerge, but it's pretty remarkable and worth noting if this is your interest:

Lesson 5: Ever read that book *The Secret*? Have you had trouble making it work for you? I'm finding that once you get the clutter out of your being, it is much easier and more second nature to start bringing people, places and situations into your life that are not only beneficial, but also truly magical. Some call that "the power of positive thinking." I call what I've found on my journey this summer "the power of positive *being*."

In recapturing that positive being, I've also regained 43 minutes of time each day (that is, my pings of the virtual world are down from 530+ a day to only 10 or 12). I've grown beyond the Pavlovian response to the blinking green light on my Droid, and will neither salivate nor turn it back on in the future. And the world is safer with one less driver texting and tweeting in traffic, because *I can wait, and so can you*. The world can unfold for me now in its own time; I'm not going to *push* to fold it. My encouragement to self to "take it one day at a time" is no longer necessary, because all days have become the same day.

Remember when I wondered if anyone would notice that I was "gone" from the virtual world? My ego is pleased to announce that my absence did not go entirely unnoticed. One friend confessed that she was reluctant to get in touch with me to ask what happened (in case my recent events were embarrassingly life changing, or if I had died). I let her know that if I *had* died, I wouldn't have even responded to her message. She admitted that she realized that, but "you know, so many people mysteriously drop offline when they're going through major problems in life, and I just didn't want to ask." So Dear Friends: I am neither dead (to my knowledge), nor newly divorced or split or re-partnered, nor in a mental institution, nor considering abandoning life as I know it and moving to a foreign country. (OK, so I *have* considered that last one, but I'll hold off on action for a while.) I am, however, a freshly emerging self, hatching from its own ego and culture – which I'm sure will lead to its own surprises in the months and weeks to come. Sounds exciting, actually.

Things begin, and things end. My 21 days of disintegration have drifted into the wind, carried by ash and dust. My 21 days of re-construction have now ended as well. It's time to shift out of the paper-journal and into my new life — the one that is enhanced (and not poisoned) by my connections to technology and so-cial media. But as with all endings, I wouldn't be surprised if the story continues online. The collective unconscious has a knack, especially on the Internet, for promoting the perpetual motion of ideas. For me, what was unconscious has become conscious; the light and dark of the inner self is revealed, and I can now live more honestly and fully. It will not all be pleasant, *but it will all be real.*

> Going to leave this brokedown palace. On my hands & my knees, I will roll, roll, roll
> 11:59PM on 7/11/2010 from paper-journal

Things begin, and things end. Yet sometimes, things just continue to *evolve* in surprising ways, the snake eats its own tail, the im-possible perfections materialize with magical clarity and purpose, and you realize *it's all there all the time anyway.*

And then the train shows up.

Acknowledgements

Every person is a blend of the people, places, situations and ideas they have become entangled with throughout their lives. However, some entanglements are more profound and complex than others, and the echoes of these voices in my life are woven into many of the pages herein: @jack122112, who destroyed most of my illusions about illusions; @rduplain, who continually infuses me with philosophy about technology, productivity, and systems engineering; and @morphatic, who turns me on to new ways of being and transformative paradigms, and has catalyzed experiments in lifelong learning.

This experiment would not have been conducted without an intervention by my mother, Mary Eisele Radziwill, who confronted me with my problem and told me I had an ugly and irritating addiction. She had a little help from Oprah, who was (on that day) promoting the notion of disconnecting from technology to repair relationships.

Also thanks to Tracey Linkous Danner for helping me type, and to Tracey, Todd, @mememe4u, @morphatic and Dan Epstein for previewing the manuscript.

References

The journaling experience would not have been complete without peppering my own observations with passages from my summer reading list. Here are the major players.

Adams, D. (1979). *The Hitchhiker's guide to the galaxy*. Serious Productions, Ltd.

Csikszentmihalyi, M. (1993). *The evolving self*. New York, NY: Harper Perennial.

Dass, R. (1974). *The only dance there is: talks at the Menninger Foundation, 1970, and Spring Grove Hospital, 1972*. Garden City, NY: Anchor Press.

Good, M. D., Brodwin, P. E., Good, B. J. & Kleinman, A. (1994). *Pain as human experience: an anthropological perspective*. Berkeley, CA: University of California Press.

Moore, T. (1998). *Care of the soul: how to add depth and meaning to your everyday life*. New York, NY: HarperCollins.

Park, J. (n.d.) *Becoming more authentic: the positive side of existentialism*. Retrieved from http://www.tc.umn.edu/~parkx032/CY-AU.html

Park, J. (2007). *New ways of loving: how authenticity transforms relationships*, 6th ed. Retrieved from http://www.tc.umn.edu/~parkx032/D-NWL.html

Pink, D. (2009). *Drive: the surprising truth about what motivates us.* New York, NY: Riverhead Books.

Pirsig, R. M. (1974, 1999). *Zen and the art of motorcycle maintenance.* New York, NY: Harper Perennial Modern Classics.

Reeves, B. & Nass, C. (1996). *The media equation: how people treat computers, television, and new media like real people and places.* Stanford, CA: CSLI Publications.

Robbins, T. (1971, 1990, 2003). *Another roadside attraction.* New York, NY: Bantam Dell.

Trapani, G. (2006). *Lifehacker: 88 tech tricks to turbocharge your day.* Indianapolis, IN: Wiley Publishing, Inc.

About the Author

Nicole Radziwill is a faculty member in the Department of Integrated Science and Technology at James Madison University (JMU) in Harrisonburg, Virginia. She has a PhD in technology management with a specialization in quality systems, which is only somewhat useful in her battle with technology addiction. She is passionate about quality, continuous improvement, mindfulness, and the lifelong pursuit of *authenticity*.

Although her body lives in Charlottesville, Virginia, her heart is often stationed in Boulder, Colorado (that is, when it's not in southern Germany).

Made in the USA
Lexington, KY
07 November 2011